MURDER & MAYHEM IN
ESSEX
COUNTY

MURDER & MAYHEM IN ESSEX COUNTY

ROBERT WILHELM

Charleston  London

THE
History
PRESS

Published by The History Press
Charleston, SC 29403
www.historypress.net

Copyright © 2011 by Robert Wilhelm
All rights reserved

Front cover: Hannah Duston Monument, *photo by Peter Meo; Joseph White*, by Benjamin Blyth,
courtesy of Peabody Essex Museum.
Back cover: Map of Essex County, *by Tom Wilhelm;* Annisquam, *photo by Peter Meo.*

First published 2011

Manufactured in the United States

ISBN 978.1.60949.400.1

Library of Congress Cataloging-in-Publication Data

Wilhelm, Robert.
Murder and mayhem in Essex County / Robert Wilhelm.
p. cm.
Includes bibliographical references.
ISBN 978-1-60949-400-1
1. Murder--Massachusetts--Essex County--History. 2. Violent crimes--Massachusetts--
Essex County--History. 3. Essex County (Mass.)--History, Local. I. Title.
HV6533.M4W55 2011
364.152'3097445--dc23
011041042

CONTENTS

ACKNOWLEDGEMENTS

I would like to thank my wife, Anne, for coordinating the acquisition of pictures and other miscellaneous legwork necessary to the production of this book. Thanks to my son Tom (www.tom-wilhelm.com) for the fantastic original drawings, and thanks to Peter Meo (www.petermeophotography. com) for the excellent original photographs. And thank you to Kurt Wilhelm (no relation) for providing information on the murder of Carrie Andrews.

INTRODUCTION

J ust three years after the Pilgrims landed at Plymouth Rock, the first settlers put down roots in what would later become Essex County, Massachusetts. If the legends are true, that the Plymouth colonists lived in harmony with one another and at peace with the natives, the same cannot be said of Essex. From the earliest days, life in Essex County reads like an adventure book filled with Indian fighters, highwaymen, pirates and witches. Even as civilization overtook Essex County in the years that followed, a frontier spirit remained in certain quarters, where murder and mayhem were the order of the day.

Of course, violence had existed in that corner of the world long before the English arrived—the native Agawam tribe periodically fought off attacks from the Tarrantines, a rival tribe from the north, and the Indians had their own domestic transgressions and punishments—but the English brought with them the notion of written history. This account begins when the magistrates of the Massachusetts Bay Colony began recording dates, places, victims and criminals.

The first bit of mayhem brought by the English to the land of the Agawams occurred before white men had even settled there. Starting about 1611, the Virginia Colony sent voyages up the coast to the land they called North Virginia looking for sites for future settlement. In 1614, Captain John Smith of Virginia described the land of the Agawams:

> *Here are many rising hills, and on their tops and desents are many corne fields and delightful groues. On the east is an Isle of two or three leagues*

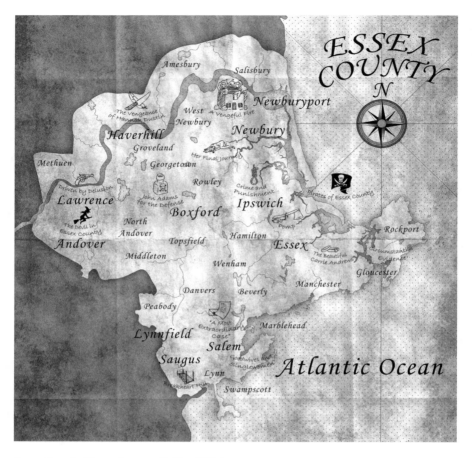

Essex County, Massachusetts. *By Tom Wilhelm.*

*in length; the one halfe plaine marish ground, fit for pasture, or salt ponds,
with many faire high groues of mulberry trees. There are also okes, pines,
walnuts, and other wood, to make this place an excellent habitation.*

The early English visitors found the natives of Agawam friendly, treating
them more kindly than had other Indian tribes. But the contact was
devastating for the Agawam tribe, which by 1617 was almost completely
wiped out by a plague, probably smallpox or hepatitis.

The Agawams remained friendly to the English as settlement of their
land began in the 1620s, but now it was out of necessity as much as natural
congeniality. In their diminished state, the Agawams had trouble defending

The deed to Ipswich signed by Masconomet. *From* A Sketch of the Life of John Winthrop the Younger.

themselves from their traditional enemies from the north. They depended on help from the English, who were now also threatened by the raiding Tarrantines. As the colonies began to grow, Masconomet, the sachem, or chief, of the Agawam tribe, remained a friend to the English, and in 1638, he agreed to sell for twenty pounds the land that would include most of Essex County.

Masconomet's death in 1658 prompted the last act of mayhem perpetrated against the Agawams by English settlers. Masconomet was buried on Sagamore Hill, in a part of Ipswich that would later become the town of Hamilton. Though Masconomet had always been a friend to the English, a gang of young rowdies dug up his remains and paraded around town with Masconomet's skull on a pole. The vandals were arrested and punished by the Town of Ipswich.

Masconomet's remains were reburied on Sagamore Hill, but the incident distressed the tribe—by their religion, disturbing the grave had caused the spirit of Masconomet to return to roam the earth until the proper ceremony was performed. This ceremony was not performed until 1993, when Oee-

Masconomet's grave today. *Photo by Peter Meo.*

Tash, chief of the Ponkapoag tribe on Cape Cod, performed the sacred ceremony. Today, Masconomet shares Sagamore Hill with a U.S. Air Force radio observatory. His grave is in a secluded section of the hill but is open to the public. People who visit the site leave tributes of photographs, dream catchers and other handmade decorations.

With the exception of the story of Hannah Dustin's capture by, and escape from, the Abenaki Indians—a particularly violent and controversial tale of Essex County murder and mayhem—all the stories in this book involve settlers from abroad and their descendants. I begin this account with the earliest murders occurring in the Puritan settlements in Essex. Although information is sparse, it is clear that these cases had a powerful impact on the community. The facts come from public records and from the diaries and histories written by patriarchs such as John Winthrop and Cotton Mather. Where direct quotes are included, I have kept the original spelling, punctuation and capitalization, inserting missing words only when absolutely necessary to preserve the meaning. As in other modern accounts, I have used standardized spelling of proper names, though they may have been spelled differently in documents at the time.

The Puritans came to the New World to found a perfect community based on righteousness and strict adherence to their interpretation of God's law.

For this to work, the entire community needed to share Puritan beliefs, and this became increasingly difficult to enforce in the new settlements. The first murders in Essex County occurred within ten years of the earliest settlement and were perpetrated by outsiders—William Schooler, a marginal character who came to America to flee prosecution for crimes in Europe, and John Williams, a ship carpenter from England who probably would have returned had he not been arrested in Boston for theft. While the first killers came from outside the community, it was not long before the harsh conditions and the strict laws of the Puritans drove some of their own community to murder. Dorothy Talbye and Elizabeth Emerson were Puritan women who, in two separate cases, murdered their own children.

The most egregious murders in Essex County—and the most startling example of mass hysteria in American history—were the executions, by law, of twenty people for witchcraft in Salem Village. The Salem witch trials have been so well documented and so thoroughly analyzed that a casual observer is left with the impression that this was an isolated incident, beginning and ending in one place during one discrete period of time. This is not true. In the chapter on witchcraft, I briefly summarize the events in Salem Village that triggered the madness, but I expand the focus to look at the roots of witchcraft throughout Essex County decades earlier and the effects of the trials in other communities—particularly the town of Andover, which had significantly more accused witches than Salem Village.

In the eighteenth century, as Puritan dominance faded, the citizens of Essex County had other concerns. The growth of shipbuilding, fishing and maritime trade in the harbors of Cape Ann in Essex County inevitably led to the scourge of piracy along the coast. I have included three very different stories of swashbuckling along the shores of Essex, none of which ends happily for the pirates.

In addition to those perils unique to the North Shore of Massachusetts, following the American Revolution, Essex County faced problems common to all the growing regions in the new republic. The fires that devastated many of America's major cities in the nineteenth century came early to the city of Newburyport. In 1811, sixteen and a half acres of densely built commercial and residential property were completely destroyed. When a second major fire, nine years later, was proven to be the work of an arsonist, the people of Newburyport would have their revenge.

The unique and often ambiguous status of slavery in Massachusetts led to tragedy in the town of Andover. A young slave named Pomp decided to take revenge against a cruel master when, by law, he could have just walked away.

Massachusetts, in the colonial period and early days of the United States, was famous for its statesmen and legal minds. I have included two stories of celebrity lawyers arguing cases in the county courthouse in Salem. Before achieving fame as one of the nation's founding fathers, a young attorney named John Adams defended an accused murderer in a controversial case of poisoning in the town of Boxford. In 1830, the prominent lawyer, orator and sitting U.S. senator Daniel Webster was hired to prosecute a particularly difficult murder case in the city of Salem.

By the end of the nineteenth century, Essex County would experience the same types of sensational murder that were dominating newspaper headlines across America. In the city of Lawrence, Henry Goodwin would plead temporary insanity to the blatant murder of a business associate. Alfred C. Williams would be charged with a murder in Lynnfield on evidence so circumstantial that his attorney could argue that no crime had been committed. And a love story involving a beautiful young singer from the town of Essex would end in tragedy. I will close with the trial of John C. Best for the murder of George E. Bailey in 1900. It was the last Essex County murder of the nineteenth century and the first for which the prosecution would seek execution by the electric chair.

Essex is one of the oldest counties in America. In the 277 years between the first settlement and the turn of the twentieth century, murder and mayhem were never far from the lives of its citizens. While founded as a new world of Christian righteousness, and priding itself on civility and the rule of law, Essex County's history is as bloody and barbaric as that of any part of America. But establishing a new country in a harsh land sometimes calls for harsh measures, and we can take pride in the fact that, more often than not, justice prevailed.

HER FINAL JOURNEY
NEWBURY, 1636

In the autumn of 1636, an Agawam Indian walking through the Winnacunnet woods, north of the town of Newbury, found the body of a young white woman lying in a thick swamp about three miles north of the Merrimack River. From the condition of the body, he could tell that the woman had been dead for several months. She lay naked, with her clothing still in a pile not far from the body. The Indian took the news to Newbury and led the Englishmen to the spot so they could see for themselves.

The woman's name was Mary Sholy. She was identified more by the circumstance than by appearance, since the flesh had begun to rot. Mary had left Newbury several months earlier, traveling north to her home at the English settlement at Pascataquack. The people of Newbury were also fairly certain who had killed her; they believed she had been ravished and murdered by the man she had hired to guide her journey home, an outsider named William Schooler.

Newbury had been a town for just over a year, but it was rapidly growing. In 1633, John Winthrop, governor of the Massachusetts Bay Colony, charged his son John to begin Puritan settlements in Agawam, the land north of Salem, "least an enemy finding it void should possess and take it from us." Within a year, Agawam (renamed Ipswich) became part of the colony, and in 1635, the town of Newbury, formerly known as Quascacunquen, was officially incorporated.

Land was granted to colonists in England who began to settle in Ipswich and Newbury. By law, no one was allowed to inhabit a town without the

Discovering the body of Mary Sholy. *By Tom Wilhelm.*

express consent of its freemen. A man could be made a freeman by the general court if he was a church member, was not in debt and was not idle. Only freemen could vote for magistrates or hold office. All freemen were required to take the Freemen's Oath:

> *I, _ _, being by God's providence an inhabitant and freeman within the jurisdiction of this Commonwealth, do freely acknowledge myself to be subject to the government thereof, and therefore do swear by the great and dreadful name of the everlasting God, that I will be true and faithful to the same, and will accordingly yield assistance and support thereunto, with my person and estate, as in equity I am bound; and I will also truly endeavour*

to maintain and preserve all the liberties and privileges thereof, submitting myself to the wholesome laws and orders, made and established by the same. And further, that I will not plot nor practice any evil against it, nor consent to any, that shall so do, but will truly discover and reveal the same to lawful authority now here established, for the speedy preventing thereof. Moreover, I do solemnly bind myself in the sight of God, that when I shall be called to give my voice and suffrage, as I shall judge in mine own conscience may best conduce and tend to public weal of the body, without respect of persons or favor of any man; so help me God in the Lord Jesus Christ.

Residents who were not freemen remained in town only with the permission of the freemen and, after six months, were required to swear a Residents' Oath, requiring them to be "obedient and conformable" to the authority of the town and governor. They would receive the protection of the laws but not the rights of freemen. But not everyone arriving from England lived up to the Christian standards demanded by the Puritans. Those who were not freemen or formal residents of the town were encouraged to stay away.

William Schooler was exactly the kind of person whom the law intended to keep out of Newbury. In London, England, Schooler had been a vintner with intemperate habits. Though he had been married to "a handsome, neat woman," Schooler was, by his own admission, a common adulterer. After wounding a man in a duel, he fled to Holland to escape the law. Then, leaving his wife behind, he traveled to New England. In 1636, he was living in a shack by the Merrimack River within the limits of Newbury but outside the boundaries of sanctioned Christian behavior.

Mary Sholy, a servant girl, was looking for someone to guide her to Pascataquack to return to her master. Pascataquack (or Pascataqua)—now Portsmouth, New Hampshire—was a small settlement about twenty-three miles north of Newbury. It is not known why Mary Sholy had come to Newbury. She may have been visiting friends or relatives; it is unlikely that her master would have sent her there without providing a guide back. The journey from Newbury to Pascataquack would have been too perilous for a young woman to take alone, first crossing the Merrimack River in a canoe and then following the route to Pascataquack, which was described as little more than a path through the woods. In 1636, even the well-traveled path between Ipswich and Newbury was too narrow for a horse cart. In addition to the possibility of losing her way and becoming hopelessly lost in the woods between the two settlements, there was a very real danger of being attacked by wild animals or hostile Indians.

Seeing an opportunity to make a little money, William Schooler sought out Mary and offered to guide her home for fifteen shillings. He did not tell her that he himself had never made the trip to Pascataquack before. Two days after their departure, William Schooler was back in Newbury alone. When asked why he had returned so soon, Schooler replied that he had guided Mary to within two or three miles of Pascataquack, where she stopped, saying she would go no farther. Schooler left her there and returned to Newbury.

The people of Newbury remained suspicious, and Schooler was questioned by the magistrates in Ipswich. When he returned from the trip, he had blood on his hat and a scratch on his nose the "breadth of a small nail." He explained that the blood was from a pigeon he had killed and the scratch on his nose was from walking into some brambles. He was released, as there was no evidence then that a crime had been committed.

The following year, the Pequod tribe took up arms against the English colonists, and Schooler was drafted to serve in the militia. He deemed this service to be an oppression and publicly spoke out against it. His outspoken opposition was considered "mutinous and disorderly," and the governor issued a warrant against him. Schooler did not know about the warrant, and when he was arrested, he assumed he would be questioned again about Mary Sholy. He began to vehemently defend himself against the charge of her murder. Schooler's behavior made the magistrates suspicious, and since they now knew Mary Sholy had been murdered, they decided to reopen the case.

Newbury residents who knew him came forward to volunteer information on Schooler's character. In a Puritan court, the character of the accused was as important as the physical evidence against him. Here is the evidence against John Schooler as outlined by Governor John Winthrop in his book *The History of New England from 1630 to 1649*:

> *1. He had lived a vicious life, and now lived like an atheist.*
> *2. He had sought out the maid, and undertook to carry her to a place, where he had never been.*
> *3. When he crossed Merrimack, he landed in a place three miles from the usual path from whence it was scarce possible she should get onto the path.*
> *4. He said he went by the Winicowett house, which he said stood on the contrary side of the way.*

5. Being, as he said, within two or three miles of Swamscote, where he left her, he went not thither to tell them of her, nor staid by her that night, nor, at his return home, did tell any body of her till he was demanded of her.

6. When he came back, he had above ten shillings in his purse, and yet he said she would give him but seven shillings, and he carried no money with him.

7. At his return he had some blood upon his hat, and on his skirts before, which he said was with a pigeon, which he killed.

8. He had a scratch on the left side of his nose, and, being asked by a neighbor how it came, he said it was with a bramble, which it could not be, it being of the breadth of a small nail; and being asked after by the magistrate, he said it was with his piece, but that could not be on the left side.

9. The body of the maid was found by an Indian, about half a year after, in the midst of a thick swamp, ten miles abort of the place he said he left her in, and about three mile from the place where he landed by Merrimack, (and it was after seen by the English,) the flesh being rotted of it, and the clothes laid all on a heap by the body.

10. He said that, soon after he left her, he met with a bear, and he thought that bear might kill her, yet he would not go back to save her.

11. He brake prison, and fled as far as Powder Horn Hill and there hid himself out of the way, for fear of pursuit and after, when he arose to go forward, he could not, but (as himself confessed) was force to return back to prison again.

Schooler denied that he had murdered Mary Sholy, but the jury found him guilty, and he was sentenced to hang. The court and the clergy tried desperately to persuade Schooler to confess, but he would not. Schooler was contrite at his execution, saying he had told many lies to excuse himself, but he vehemently denied that he had killed or ravished Mary Sholy. Some ministers and others argued that the evidence against him was not sufficient to take away his life, but Governor Winthrop disagreed and denied Schooler a reprieve, saying: "But the court held him worthy of death, in undertaking the charge of a shiftless maid, and leaving her (when he might have done otherwise) in such a place, as he knew she must needs parish, if not preserved by means unknown."

William Schooler was sentenced to hang on September 28, 1637.

CRIME AND PUNISHMENT
WENHAM/IPSWICH, 1637

The Scarlet Letter, by Salem author Nathaniel Hawthorne, was set in a Puritan Massachusetts village in 1642. In the book, young Hester Prynne is forced to wear the letter "A" on her breast as a badge of shame for her sin of adultery. This type of punishment—shaming the convicted criminal—was common in the towns of Essex County in the seventeenth century. While punishment might also include whipping, branding or imprisoning the sinner, public humiliation was always as important as physical pain.

On September 3, 1633, an inhabitant of Ipswich was sentenced to pay twenty pounds and stand with "a white sheet of paper on his back whereon 'Drunkard' is written in great letters" for "abusing himself shamefully with drink and enticing his neighbor's wife to incontinency and other misdemeanors."

On March 5, 1639, a person was severely whipped in Boston and Ipswich and forced to wear the letter "V" on his outer garment for the crime of "lewd attempts."

On April 15, 1684, a Salem man, convicted twice before of theft, was convicted of burglary in Ipswich and sentenced to be branded with a "B," to pay treble damages and to be whipped fifteen lashes in Salem on the next lecture day.

Other common modes of punishment used in Ipswich were:

Crime and Punishment

The hanging of William Schooler and John Williams, September 28, 1637. *By Tom Wilhelm.*

- Stocks: Where the prisoner's feet are immobilized between two boards in a public place to be taunted by those who pass by.
- Pillory: Similar to stocks, the prisoner—usually someone who had "made haste to be rich by fraudulent practices"—must stand with his head and hands locked between two boards. Sometimes one or both ears would be clipped to mark the offense.
- Cage: A cage, about ten feet by sixteen feet, to hold Sabbath-breakers and other transgressors on lecture days so they would be exposed to the whole congregation.
- Cleft stick: To confine the tongue of convicted slanderers.
- Ducking and gagging: For the crime of "exorbitancy of the tongue in railing and scolding," it was ordered that "railers and scolds be gagged or set in a ducking-stool, and dipped in water, over head and ears three times."

Punishments were administered in the community where the criminal lived to maximize the humiliation. The exception to this rule was the punishment of capital crimes. No matter where the crimes were committed, executions took place publicly, on Boston Common, for the edification of the entire colony. Executions were solemn occasions, used by the clergy as

Stocks and pillory. *Photo by Peter Meo.*

an opportunity for moral instruction. They were always accompanied by a stern sermon.

On September 28, 1637, two men convicted in Essex County on separate counts of murder were executed in Boston at the same time, on the same gallows. The first was William Schooler, convicted a year earlier of killing Mary Sholy on the path to Pascataquack; the second was John Williams, convicted of killing John Hoddy near Great Pond in Wenham.

John Williams was a ship carpenter who had recently come to America from England. In 1637, he was in prison in Boston for theft. Williams and another prisoner, John Hoddy, escaped from the jail and traveled north. They had gone beyond Salem and were on the road to Ipswich, on the east end of the Wenham Great Pond—now called Wenham Lake—when they had a falling out. The two men had a fight that ended with the death of John Hoddy.

There are two versions of what happened next. In one story, John Hoddy's dog held Williams at bay until the noise drew the attention of enough residents of Wenham to apprehend Williams and take him to jail in Ipswich. The more likely story says that Williams took everything belonging to Hoddy, including his clothes, and buried his body under a pile of stones.

Wenham Lake (Great Pond). *Photo by Peter Meo.*

Williams proceeded to Ipswich, where he was apprehended after being recognized as a criminal. Though his clothes were bloody when arrested, he would confess to nothing until a week later, when the body of John Hoddy was found. Cows at a farm near Great Pond smelled the blood and made such a "roaring" that they got the attention of the cow keeper, who, on investigation, found Hoddy's naked body under a heap of stones.

Around the same time, the justice of the peace in Ipswich learned that both Williams and Hoddy were escaped prisoners. Williams was indicted for the murder of John Hoddy and tried by the court of assistants in Boston. Though he confessed to the murder, the court insisted on enforcing Williams's right to due process and tried the case before a jury. Williams was, of course, found guilty and sentenced to death.

The double hanging in Boston of William Schooler and John Williams was an event significant enough to be immortalized in John Winthrop's *History of New England 1630 to 1649* and has been retold in numerous Essex County town histories.

GOODWIVES AND SINGLEWOMEN
ESSEX COUNTY, 1638–1725

In Puritan Massachusetts, a married woman was addressed as "goodwife," often shortened to "goody"; an unmarried woman was a "singlewoman." While the moral laws of the Puritans could sometimes seem complex, a woman's role in society can be very simply expressed: the duty of a goodwife is to bear children; the duty of a singlewoman is to not bear children.

As simple as this rule seemed, it was not always easy to follow. In addition to the hardships of the American wilderness and the austerity of the church, married women sometimes buckled under the demands of tyrannical husbands, the rigors of almost constant pregnancy and the trials of raising good Puritan children. Singlewomen, unable to suppress natural urges, would succumb to seduction, and if the outcome was pregnancy, the consequences could be devastating for all involved. In both cases, the desperate women sometimes turned to murdering their own children. Given how unnatural this crime is in any culture, it was surprisingly common in the rigidly moral society of the Massachusetts Bay Colony.

Dorothy Talbye (also spelled Talbie) was a goodwife of Salem, noted for her esteem and Godliness. She lived with her husband, John Talbye, and their four children on a farm so small it could barely support them. Around the time of the birth of her fourth child, Dorothy became depressed and despondent. This condition manifested itself in the name she gave her new daughter. It was common among Puritans to name babies, particularly girls, after virtuous traits, such as Constant, Gracious, Hopeful. Dorothy named her little girl Difficult.

A Fair Puritan, by E. Percy Moran.
Wikimedia Commons.

Her condition worsened, and Dorothy began to quarrel with her husband, her neighbors and clergymen. Believing that she could hear the word of God directly, Dorothy stopped attending church. God told her to stop eating meat and to stop feeding her family. Then she turned violent, assaulting her husband and on one occasion attempting to murder him. In 1637, she was brought before the magistrates in Salem, who ordered:

> *Whereas Dorothy the wyfe of John Talbie hath not only broak that peace & Love which ought to have beene both betwixte them, but also hath violentlie broke the kings peace, by frequent Laying hands upon hir husband to the danger of his Life, & Contemned Authority, not coming before them upon command, It is therefore ordered that for hir misdemeanor passed & for prevention of future evills that are feared willbe committed by hir if shee be Lefte att hir Libertie. That she shall be bound & chained to some post where shee shall be restrained of hir libertye to goe abroad or comminge to hir husband till shee manifest some change of hir course.*

But Dorothy did not change her course. As a result of continuing to defy authority and physically assaulting her husband, Dorothy Talbye was excommunicated from the church. In 1638, she was again found guilty of misdemeanor against her husband and was publicly whipped. According to Governor Winthrop, "She reformed for a time, and carried herself more dutifully to her husband." But it did not last; that November, she once again fell victim to "spiritual delusions." Believing that she was acting at the persuasion of God, Dorothy broke the neck of her three-year-old daughter, Difficult, killing her. Dorothy said she had done it to spare her daughter future misery.

When charged with the murder, Dorothy readily confessed, insisting that she just wanted to make sure the child did not live a life of poverty. The court of assistants, however, refused to accept the confession made while being interrogated, fearing it had been wrung out under duress. But at her arraignment, when she was urged to plead guilty, Dorothy became belligerent, refusing to enter a plea of any kind until threatened with *peine forte et dure*—the practice of placing heavy stones on the prisoner's chest until he or she either cooperated or died. She finally pleaded guilty and requested beheading for her execution, because she said it was less painful and less shameful than hanging. Dorothy was sentenced by Governor Winthrop to hang.

Dorothy Talbye remained defiant to the end; she refused to repent, taunting the crowd that had gathered on Boston Common on December 6, 1638, to witness the hanging. She removed the black hood from her head and put it around her neck to make the noose less painful. When the support was pulled away and she was hanging from the gallows, she tried, after a swing or two, to grab the ladder with her feet but failed. Dorothy Talbye was the first woman executed in Massachusetts.

SINGLEWOMEN

The Emersons of Haverhill were the kind of family that just could not stay out of trouble. Michael and Hannah Emerson were among the early settlers but were not founding members of the town. Michael took a number of menial commercial and municipal jobs and at one point moved from the outskirts into the center of Haverhill. But Michael's reputation was poor, and the family was not welcomed in town. The town magistrates persuaded Michael and his family to "go back to the woods" by giving the Emersons an additional tract of land.

Michael Emerson's first child, Hannah, would marry Thomas Duston and, in the eyes of many, redeem the family name by her heroism in the face of Indian captivity, but that would be many years and many sins later. Death was a common feature in the Emerson household; only nine of their fifteen children survived infancy. The sixth child was a daughter named Elizabeth, born in 1664. In May 1676, Michael was brought to court "for cruel and excessive beating of his daughter with a flail swingle and for kicking her, and was fined and bound to good behavior." The daughter was twelve-year-old Elizabeth. Corporal punishment was not considered wrong in and of itself, but Michael's beating of Elizabeth was criminally excessive. There is no way to know why Elizabeth was being punished, but the impression is that she was a rambunctious, strong-willed child living in a violent household.

Another of Elizabeth's sisters, Mary Emerson, was married in 1683 to Hugh Mathews of Newbury. Though there is no record of premature offspring, Hugh and Mary were both brought to court and found guilty of fornication before marriage. They were sentenced to be "fined or severely whipped."

Perhaps with her sister as an example, Elizabeth also engaged in premarital sex. In 1686, Elizabeth Emerson gave birth to an illegitimate daughter she named Dorothy. It is not clear whether Elizabeth was ever punished for this, but court records indicate that Michael Emerson accused a neighbor, Timothy Swan, of being the father. Timothy's father, Robert Swan, vehemently denied that Timothy was the father because he "had charged him not to go into that wicked house and his son had obeyed and furthermore his son could not abide the jade." He further threatened to "carry the case to Boston" if Timothy were formally accused. Michael did not pursue the charges, and little Dorothy remained fatherless.

Five years later, with Elizabeth and her daughter still living at her parents' house, Elizabeth became pregnant again. She somehow managed to keep this a secret from her parents, but the neighbors were suspicious. Sometime during the night of May 7, 1691, Elizabeth, who slept at the foot of the bed where her mother and father slept, gave birth to twins without waking her parents. The twins were either stillborn or murdered by their mother. She hid the bodies in a trunk for three days and then sewed them into a sack and buried them in the backyard.

The following Sunday, while her parents were at church, the neighbors who had suspected Elizabeth's pregnancy came to the house with a warrant from the magistrates of Haverhill. While the women examined Elizabeth, the men went to the backyard and found the bodies buried in a shallow grave. Elizabeth was arrested for murdering her bastard infants.

Elizabeth maintained that she had kept the pregnancy and birth a secret out of fear. Her mother had been suspicious, but whenever she was asked about it, Elizabeth denied she was pregnant. Michael claimed he had no idea that Elizabeth was pregnant but this time put the blame on Samuel Ladd, age forty-two, a married man nine years older than Elizabeth. Elizabeth also named Samuel Ladd as the father, saying that the "begetting" had taken place at an inn house. She also stated that Ladd was the only man with whom she had ever slept, implying that Dorothy was Ladd's daughter as well.

Although Samuel Ladd had been previously found guilty of a misdemeanor and fined for an earlier episode involving sexual advances on a younger woman, Ladd was never questioned in Elizabeth Emerson's case. Elizabeth was already the mother of a bastard child, and Samuel Ladd was the son of an early settler—her story was not believed.

Elizabeth Emerson was sentenced to hang and remanded to the custody of the Boston prison on May 13, 1691. An accompanying letter explained the facts and said that she had been examined for "whore-dom." By English law, concealment of the death of a bastard child had been punishable by execution. Though this law had been repealed in England, it was still on the books in Massachusetts. It did not matter whether Elizabeth Emerson had murdered her babies or merely concealed their death—she would be hanged.

The hanging was scheduled for 1693. Although this was during the height of the Salem witch trials, in which the Reverend Cotton Mather played an active role, he found time to take an interest in Elizabeth Emerson's case. Mather worked on her soul, and before her execution, Elizabeth confessed that "when they were born, I was not unsensible, that at least one of them was alive; but such a Wretch was I, as to use a Murderous Carriage towards them, in the place where I lay, on purpose to dispatch them out of the World." But Mather believed she had more to confess and held little hope for her salvation.

Elizabeth Emerson was hanged in Boston on June 8, 1693, along with a black indentured servant named Grace. Before the execution, Cotton Mather preached a sermon during which he read the following declaration written by Elizabeth:

> *I am a Miserable Sinner; and I have Justly Provoked the Holy God to leave me unto that Folly of my own Heart, for which I am now Condemned to Dy…I believe, the chief thing that hath, brought me, into my present Condition, is my Disobedience to my Parents: I despised all their Godly Counsils and Reproofs; and I was always an Haughty and Stubborn*

Cotton Mather, by Peter Pelnham. *Wikimedia Commons*.

Spirit. So that now I am become a dreadful Instance of the Curs of God belonging to Disobedient Children.

There were a number of other cases of infanticide in Puritan Massachusetts, including two notable cases in Essex County. On July 31, 1701, a young woman from Newbury named Esther Rogers was executed for drowning her baby in the pond behind the first meetinghouse. Nothing is known of the father except that he was African. She confessed that it was her second illegitimate child; the first had been secreted, and she did not know if it was alive or dead.

At her execution, Esther also cited disobedience to her parents as the root of her troubles. She was hanged at Pingrey's Plain in Ipswich. On her way to the gallows, Esther had been in deep distress over her sins, but upon passing a hill, "she was divinely enabled to cast her soul upon Christ and to enjoy the consolations of a hope in him." From that time, the hill was called Comfort Hill.

In 1725, a singlewoman from Ipswich named Elizabeth Atwood was hanged for murdering her child. She went to the gallows unrepentant and unafraid. For the hanging, she dressed herself in her shabbiest clothes, knowing that by tradition the hangman kept the clothes of the person he executed. She laughed as she approached the gallows. When asked why, she said, "I am laughing to think what sorry suits the hangman will get from me."

THE DEVIL IN ESSEX COUNTY
1692

Without a doubt, the most nefarious events ever to take place in Essex County were the trials and executions of twenty women and men, and the imprisonment of dozens more, between 1692 and 1693 for practicing witchcraft. The witch trials in Salem Village (now the town of Danvers) have become synonymous with mass hysteria and injustice and have left an indelible stain on the reputation of Salem, Massachusetts. The notion of accusing and punishing witches has become so tightly bound to Salem as to leave the impression that it was an isolated incident, a brief moment of insanity limited to that place and time, ending as suddenly as it began. In fact, accusations of witchcraft had a long history in Essex County that neither began nor ended in Salem.

The Puritan worldview included many unseen entities and forces; they were surrounded by devils and demons, as well as the presence of God. Everything that happened in the physical world was a manifestation either of God's will or the influence of the devil. If a man had a toothache, it was evidence that he had somehow sinned with his teeth. If a cow took sick, it was likely possessed by a demon. People, as well, were either following the will of the Lord or were under the devil's influence. Sometimes the devil's presence in a man or woman was too pronounced to be overlooked. As early as 1652, forty years before the Salem trials, a man in Ipswich was sentenced to pay twenty shillings or be whipped for "having familiarity with the devil."

In the decade before the witch trials, the Reverend John Hale twice had to deal with charges of witchcraft in the town of Beverly. Dorcas Hoar, known to own a book on palmistry, was believed to have advanced to more serious sorcery. Bridget Bishop, who owned two taverns and was fond of wearing a "red paragon bodice" trimmed in lace, was accused of malefaction in the death of a neighbor. Both of these women had been "cried out" as witches by residents of Beverly, but Reverend Hale was slow to believe them evil and used his influence to clear the charges.

Salem witch trials. *By Tom Wilhelm.*

For many years, Wilmot Redd (sometimes spelled Reed), known as Mammy, was feared as a witch in the town of Marblehead. Mammy Redd was believed to have a malignant touch and sight, which she used to cast spells over those she wished to injure. She allegedly could bring sickness and death by merely wishing that a "bloody cleaver" might be found in the cradle of an infant child. One Marblehead woman claimed that she could not urinate for two weeks after being cursed by Mammy Redd. And, most notably, Mammy Redd had the ability to curdle milk and turn butter to "blue wool," a trait that inspired this bit of rhyme:

> *Old Mammy Redd*
> *Of Marblehead,*
> *Sweet milk could turn*
> *To mould in churn*

Prior to the Salem trials, the most notorious witch in Essex County was Susana Martin of Amesbury, who was first brought to court on charges of witchcraft in 1669 for allegedly bewitching a neighbor. The charges were dropped, but stories of her evil powers continued for the next twenty-three years. John Allen had put out fourteen head of cattle to feed on the salt grass at Salisbury Beach. The cows ran away from him "with violence…wholly diabolic" and were goaded by the devil to swim to Plum Island and then out to sea. Only one cow came to her senses and returned to shore. At first, Allen wondered what sin he had committed to earn God's punishment, but then he remembered that he had refused to hitch his ox cart to haul staves for Susana Martin and in a shrill, spiteful voice she had said, "Your oxen will never do you much service." Surely, it was Susana who had sent the devil into his cattle.

People in Amesbury believed that Susana Martin had the ability to change her shape at will. One woman saw her melt into empty space and then materialize in the form of birds that "pecked and pinched." She appeared to Robert Downs as a cat and would have killed him if he had not driven her off by saying, "Avoid, thou she-devil! In the name of God, the Father, the Son and the Holy Ghost, avoid!"

In general, even when a community believed there were witches in their midst, the suspects were seldom charged and, if charged, were seldom prosecuted. There was a Catch-22 in prosecuting witches under Puritan law: the testimony of those bewitched was the "devil's evidence" and could not be trusted. But when the door was opened by the Salem trials, all of these women—Dorcas Hoar, Bridget Bishop, Mammy Redd and Susana Martin—were tried, convicted and sentenced to hang.

So what happened in Salem Village in 1692 to change things so drastically? In May 1692, the Reverend Henry Gibbs, a visiting minister from Watertown, watched the trial of Andover's Martha Carrier, charged with being the "Queen of Hell." After witnessing her accusers alternate between trancelike drones and earsplitting shrieks, with the queen herself refuting the charges in a voice even louder, he wrote in his diary, "Wonders I saw, but how to judge and conclude I am at a loss." Three hundred years later, we are still at a loss to conclude the root cause of the hysteria in Salem, but the steps leading up to it are well recorded.

It began in the home of the Reverend Samuel Parris. Reverend Parris had spent some time in Barbados and had come to Salem Village with two slaves: Tituba, a woman who was probably part African and part Native American, and her husband, John Indian. While not as common in New England as it was in the southern plantations, slavery was not against Puritan law, and many wealthy households employed slave labor.

Reverend Parris's nine-year-old daughter Elizabeth (called Betty) and her cousin, seventeen-year-old Abigail Williams, who also lived with the Parrises, loved to listen to Tituba talk of her life in Barbados. The girls, especially Abigail, would push her to talk of spells, charms and the superstitions of her homeland. Abigail was probably most interested in fortunetelling which, though forbidden, was somewhat in vogue in the Puritan community at the time. A number of women were indulging in what Cotton Mather called, "little sorceries," using sieves, scissors and candles to foretell the future. Books of palmistry were also in circulation among the otherwise righteous Puritan women of Essex County.

As word of their talks with Tituba spread among the adolescent girls of Salem Village, the circle grew to include at least eight more girls ranging in age from twelve to twenty, as well as three married women. Just what they were learning from Tituba is not known, but it was certainly not knowledge of the Lord. The girls formed a tight bond of secrecy and were closer to one another than they were to anyone else.

Betty and Abigail began exhibiting aberrant behavior during prayers in the Parris home. Reverend Parris noticed that Betty was not bowing her head but sitting in a trancelike state. When he admonished her, she began to bark like a dog. Abigail's symptoms were even more extreme; she would get down on all fours and, while barking and braying like an animal, hide under the furniture and sometimes go into convulsions. When the Lord's Prayer

Tituba and the Children, by Alfred Fredericks. *Wikimedia Commons*.

was begun, Betty would scream at the top of her lungs, and Abigail would cover her ears and stamp her feet to drown out the words.

The Parrises tried to keep the problem to themselves, but word of Betty and Abigail's strange behavior quickly spread, and as it did, as if by contagion, the behavior would manifest itself in the homes of other members of their circle. First, Mary Walcott and Susana Sheldon suffered convulsions at the Walcott house, then Ann Putnam, then Ann and Mercy Lewis. This continued until there were afflicted girls in all parts of Salem Village.

Unable to explain the phenomenon, Reverend Parris called in a medical professional. Dr. Griggs examined Betty and Abigail, and after ruling out epilepsy and all other ailments in his limited repertoire, he declared that "the evil hand is on them."

The girls' behavior became more public and more extreme as they interrupted church services and prayer meetings. But now that they knew the girls were bewitched, the people of Salem Village were less concerned with the girls' behavior than they were with finding out who had bewitched them. The afflicted girls remained silent on this; though they were pressured to talk, they would not say who was responsible. Finally Betty, who had been the most conflicted, believing herself already damned, blurted out Tituba's name. Once Betty had broken, all the girls said Tituba, but they added the names of two women who were generally disliked by the community: Sarah Good and Sarah Osborn.

On February 29, 1692, the women were arrested, even Sarah Osborn, who was bedridden at the time. They all pled innocent, but the afflicted girls were present at their hearing and went into convulsions when the accused women spoke. Tituba was beaten by her master when she denied the charges, but eventually she learned to give the white men what they wanted to hear. She admitted to being a witch and said that the devil had asked her to serve him with four other women; two of the four were Good and Osborn. She also told of a ride they had all taken on a stick or pole. This was enough; all three were sent to jail in Ipswich.

Then the hysteria began. Martha Corey, who had expressed skepticism over the girls' bewitchment, was called out as a witch. Rebecca Nurse, previously considered among the most righteous women in Salem Village, was accused. Then Dorcas Good, a little girl between four and five years old, was condemned. The charges continued as more and more residents of Salem Village were arrested for witchcraft. The accused were strongly pressured to confess, and those who did not confess ran the risk of having all their female relatives arrested as well.

The Witch No. 1, by Joseph E. Baker. *Wikimedia Commons.*

Those who did confess fared better than those who did not. The accused witches and wizards who did not confess were brought to trial, and all who were tried were found guilty and sentenced to death. On June 10, 1692, Sarah Bishop was hanged on Gallows Hill in Salem Village. On July 19, five more visited Gallows Hill: Rebecca Nurse, Sarah Good, Elizabeth How, Sarah Wild and Susana Martin. Giles Corey, in his eighties, had been persuaded to testify against his wife, Martha, but later came to his senses and recanted his testimony. When brought to court to answer his own charges, Corey refused to speak. After failing to speak in three trials, he was taken to a field, stripped of his clothing and pressed to death by piling stones on a board placed on his body. On August 19, Martha Carrier and Reverend George Boroughs—"the king and queen of hell"—were hanged, along with four other men. On September 22, seven witches and one wizard—"eight firebrands of hell," as Reverend Nicholas Noyes called them—were hanged together on Gallows Hill.

Around the time of Martha Carrier's trial, Joseph Ballard of Andover began to suspect that his wife had been bewitched. She had been bedridden for a long time with an illness that the local doctors could not diagnose. Ballard decided he needed an outside opinion and sent for the afflicted girls of Salem Village.

Twelve-year-old Ann Putnam, accompanied by sixteen-year-old Mary Wolcott, rode to Andover on horseback. Unlike Salem Village, where a certain segment of the population had always harbored suspicions of the afflicted girls—albeit less vocally as the danger increased—in Andover, they were treated like royalty. The girls were taken to the home of Thomas Ballard to see his sick wife and then to sickrooms in other houses, and in every case, they saw the same spectral vision: one witch standing at the patient's head and another at his feet. Often when the girls reported their vision, other young people in the house would howl and convulse, claiming they saw the spirits too.

Because they were in a strange town, the girls could not identify the witches by name, so a "touch test" was proposed by a conclave of civic-minded citizens, which included Reverend Bernard and Justice of the Peace Dudley Bradstreet. In each house, the residents would be led blindfolded to the girls, who would then touch each one with their hands. If the girls gasped or trembled, the phenomenon, witnessed by all present, would prove that the person touched was a witch.

The problem for Andover was that this test returned positive results as often as not. Though at the start no one expected to find more than six or seven witches, the community now had more witches than it could handle. After signing forty arrest warrants, Justice Bradstreet declared he would sign no more, though more witches had been accused. Bradstreet himself was cried out as a wizard. Another problem was that, unlike Salem Village, where the girls began by accusing those whom the community agreed were the likeliest suspects, in Andover the girls did not know the characters of the people and were just as likely to accuse an upstanding citizen as they were an outcast.

Incredibly, most of the accused, though astonished to be exposed as witches, could not deny such compelling evidence and began searching their memories for openings they may have given the devil. Mary Osgood, whose husband was a church deacon, remembered that twelve years earlier, after the birth of her last child, she had been ill and unhappy. No doubt the devil had caught her then.

Samuel Wardwell remembered that he had sometimes said "the devil take it" when an animal got into his field. Then he recalled that at the time of his unrequited love for maid Barker, he had seen an assemblage of cats. Under further interrogation from the magistrates, Wardwell recalled that the "Prince of the Air" (Satan) had been with the cats and had made him promises, sworn him to a covenant for sixty years and baptized him in the Shaw Shin (now called Shawsheen) River.

William Barker said he had joined the devil because he had tired of the Puritans' preoccupation with damnation and found appealing the devil's promise that all men would be equal and "live bravely." He also claimed to know that there were exactly 307 practicing witches in Essex County.

But the accusations were especially hard on the most devout Puritans, who refused to lie, even to save their own lives. Ann Foster would not confess when reproached by her daughter and granddaughter for not admitting she had led them to the devil, because she knew it was not true. Mary Tyler, coerced by her brother to confess, refused, saying, "For I shall lye if I confess and who shall answer to God for my lye."

At its height, the frenzy in Andover was even greater than it was in Salem Village. Accusations continued there until October 1692, when a dog was shot to death after a convulsing Andover girl claimed that its specter had afflicted her. This was troubling to Reverend Increase Mather, who had been involved in the prosecution of witches. If the dog was actually a devil in disguise, he reasoned, no one would have been able to kill it. Since the dog had been killed, it could not have been capable of magic. The same month, some Andover girls accused "a worthy gentleman of Boston." The worthy gentleman turned around and swore out a writ against his accusers, demanding £1,000 for defamation. The threat of lawsuits effectively ended accusation of witchcraft in Andover, but not before one of its citizens had been hanged and at least fifty more were imprisoned, awaiting trial.

Also in October, the people of Salem Village began to have serious doubts about the afflicted girls when the wife of Reverend John Hale of Beverly was cried out. Hale, who had at first been reluctant to prosecute witches, had become one of the leaders of the prosecution.

But accusations still did not end. Later in October, the town of Gloucester sent for the girls. In July, the town had fought off an invasion of devils that had swarmed out of the swamp. The garrison that fought them knew they were spectral because bullets could not stop them. The afflicted girls cried out four witches in Gloucester but, upon returning to Salem, had trouble finding lodging and eventually ended up in Ipswich. In November, they were called again to Gloucester. While crossing the Ipswich Bridge, they met an old woman and went into their usual fits, accusing her of witchcraft. But Ipswich had not sent for the girls, and the people there were fed up with witchcraft; the antics were ignored. There were no further accusations.

A group of twelve citizens of Andover, led by Reverend Francis Dane, one of the few heroes of witchcraft hysteria, petitioned the governor to release, on bail, their wives and children, some as young as eight years old.

They were facing a cold winter in prisons that were old and in disrepair and were never intended to hold so many. This was followed by petitions from Topsfield, Gloucester, Haverhill and Chelmsford. Governor Phipps agreed to release those who were held only on spectral evidence; the rest he made the charge of the judges, who would be responsible for their welfare.

In January, the Massachusetts Bay Colony moved to continue the witch trials with some significant differences. The trials would not be held in Salem Village; the location would be determined by the home of the accused. And, most importantly, spectral evidence would be disallowed. Because of this rule, charges were dropped against forty-nine of the fifty-two awaiting trial. In the end, Governor Phipps pardoned the remaining three, along with everyone already convicted of witchcraft. That spring, as if waking from a long and horrible nightmare, the people of Essex County did their best to put the memory of the witch trials behind them.

THE VENGEANCE OF HANNAH DUSTON

HAVERHILL, 1697

Haverhill, in the northwest of Essex County, was first settled in 1640 and remained a frontier town for seventy years. It was surrounded by dense forest and was closer in location to hostile Indian tribes than it was to the Puritan population centers of Salem and Ipswich. Marauding wolves and Indian attacks were a constant threat, and in the early days, women did the farming as well as household drudgery, while men were engaged primarily in hunting and Indian fighting.

Though the town grew, it remained an outpost on the edge of civilization. The people of Haverhill lived in peace with the native tribes until King Philip's War in 1675. The grand sachem, or chief, of the Wampanoag tribe, Metacom, called King Philip by the English, had negotiated an alliance among most of the tribes of New England to drive out the English. While that war lasted only a year, Haverhill continued to be a target for the northern Abenaki Indians, who were aligned with the French and shared their wish to remove the English from North America. During King William's War (the first of the French and Indian Wars), from 1689 to 1697, Haverhill men went to work, and even to church, carrying loaded muskets.

The Abenaki mode of attack was to sneak quietly, cautiously approaching the enemy, and to strike when certain of catching their victim by surprise. Other times they would attack *en masse* at daybreak when the colonists were least prepared. They would steal what they could and then set fire to the houses and indiscriminately murder men, women and children. And just as distressing to survivors, they would take hostages, particularly women and children.

The vengeance of Hannah Duston. *By Tom Wilhelm.*

Abenaki couple. *Wikimedia Commons.*

The Vengeance of Hannah Duston

On March 15, 1697, Haverhill was under attack by the Abenakis. The Indians divided their force into small parties and attacked several parts of the town simultaneously. Nine houses were burned down, and twenty-seven inhabitants were killed.

Thomas Duston, a brick maker and constable in Haverhill, was working when the attack began. He grabbed his musket and mounted his horse and hurried home. As he approached the house, he ordered his seven children—ages two to seventeen—to hurry to the garrison house for safety. Seeing that it was too late to protect his house from attack, he rode after the children. Thomas had intended to pick up one of the children and ride away to guarantee that at least one child would survive the attack, but he was unable to decide which to take. Instead, with the help of the older children, he led them all to safety at the garrison house—a fortified house for protection against attack. It was probably the garrison of Onesiphorus March on Pecker's Hill.

Thomas was married to forty-year-old Hannah Emerson Duston, whose sister, Elizabeth Emerson, had been executed five years earlier for murdering her illegitimate twins. But Hannah had been a good Puritan wife, and at the time of the attack, she was at home recuperating from the birth of their twelfth child, Martha. A neighbor, Mrs. Mary Neff, was tending the week-old infant when the Indians burst into the house and took everything they could carry. They dragged Hannah, Mrs. Neff and the baby from the house with such haste that Hannah left wearing only one shoe. The attackers set fire to the house and then left, taking the three as hostages. Seeing that the baby was going to slow down their progress, the Indians seized little Martha from Mrs. Neff's arms and dashed her head against an apple tree, killing her.

In the woods outside of Haverhill, the attackers met up with the rest of their tribesmen, who had taken captives as well. In all, thirteen men, women and children of Haverhill were taken hostage by the Abenakis. Through thick forest, still showing traces of winter's snow, they traveled quickly north, following the Merrimack River. During the next few days, they covered more than one hundred miles, walking by day through the wilderness and sleeping on the frosty floor of the forest. Their plan was to march their captives north to Canada and sell them to the French as slaves.

The party stopped at an island near the junction of the Contoocook and Merrimack Rivers near what is now the town of Penacook, New Hampshire. On this island (which is now called Duston Island) was the wigwam of an Abenaki family who had been converted by the French to Catholicism. They prayed three times a day and would not let their children eat or sleep without praying. They told the captives that when they prayed the English way they thought that it was good, but they found the French way better. Also living on the island was fourteen-year-old Samuel Lennardson, who had been taken captive near Worcester, Massachusetts, about eighteen months earlier. Hannah Duston and Mary Neff were kept on the island, while the remainder of the Haverhill captives continued their march north.

Hannah Duston was determined to escape at the first opportunity. The horror of seeing her baby murdered before her eyes, along with the cruel treatment she had received on the journey, had enflamed a desire in her heart for revenge against her captors. It was fueled by stories the Indians told of how the captives would be forced to "run the gauntlet" when they reached their home in Canada. They would be stripped naked and forced to run between two rows of Indians of both sexes and endure jeers and beatings as they passed. Hannah, Mary Neff and Samuel Lennardson secretly planned their escape.

Samuel, talking casually with a member of the tribe named Bampico, asked him where he would strike a man to kill him instantly and how he would take the scalp. Pointing to his temple, Bampico said, "Strike him there!" and then proceeded to explain how to remove the scalp. The scalper places his foot on the neck of his prostrate victim and twists the fingers of his left hand into the scalp lock; then, with a knife in his right hand, he cuts a circular gash around the lock. He tears the scalp from the head and, with a yell of triumph, fastens it to his belt. Little did Bampico realize that his instructions would lead to his own demise.

From Heroism of Hannah Duston.

The night of March 30, 1697, after all their captors were asleep, Hannah, Mary and Samuel took tomahawks and all struck at once. They attacked so fast that they were able to kill ten of the Abenakis before any were able to respond. Only one woman and a boy managed to escape.

Hannah, Mary and Samuel left the wigwams carrying a tomahawk and one of the Indians' guns and hurried to the canoes. They scuttled all but one canoe and prepared to paddle it away when they realized that they would need proof of what they had done if anyone were to believe their story. They went back to their victims and, using the lesson Samuel had received from Bampico, scalped all ten of their victims and brought the scalps back to the canoe.

They traveled by night and hid by day, out of fear of being recaptured after the two Indians who escaped reported to their tribe what had happened. Finally, they saw the home of John Lovewell in Dunstable, now part of Nashua, New Hampshire. They spent the night there, continued to Bradley's Cove and then made the last leg of their journey on foot. To the surprise and joy of everyone in Haverhill, they had made it home safely.

In 1694, the Massachusetts Bay Colony had offered a bounty of fifty pounds for any Indian scalp presented to it. In 1695, the bounty was reduced to twenty-five pounds, and in December 1696, it was revoked completely. Regardless of the law, Thomas Duston believed that Hannah's heroism deserved a reward and petitioned the governor. On April 21, 1697, carrying

The Duston garrison house, Haverhill. *Photo by Peter Meo.*

Hannah Duston Monument, Monument Square, Haverhill. *Photo by Peter Meo.*

the gun, the tomahawk and the ten scalps taken from the Abenakis, Hannah and Thomas Duston traveled to Boston, where Thomas received, on Hannah's behalf, a reward of twenty-five pounds from the general court. Mary Neff and Samuel Lennardson were each given twelve pounds and ten shillings. While in Boston, Hannah told her story to the Revered Cotton Mather, who wrote about her exploits in his book *Magnalia Christi Ameriana*. Governor Nicholson of Maryland, upon hearing the story, sent Hannah an inscribed pewter tankard.

The Dustons moved into a brick house and garrison that Thomas had been working on at the time of the attack. Thomas and Hannah had one more child, Lydia, born October 4, 1698. Hannah died in 1736 at the age of seventy-nine.

Hannah Duston's heroism was commemorated by a statue in Monument Square in Haverhill in 1861 (believed to be the first public statue of a woman in America), a statue on Duston Island in 1874 and a monument at the site of John Lovewell's house in Nashua, New Hampshire. The Duston Garrison House still stands in Haverhill.

HANNAH DUSTON IN LITERATURE

Hannah Duston was considered a hero, but praise for her action has not been universal. Among the ten Abenakis killed were several children; over the years, it has been questioned whether taking their lives was necessary. The necessity of taking the scalps has also been questioned, accusing Hannah of acting out of vengeance or, worse, doing it just for the bounty.

Hannah Duston's portrayal in literature reflects this ambivalence. The story of Hannah Duston's escape captured the imagination of several nineteenth-century Massachusetts authors. All dutifully recount the captivity and escape, but each takes away a different lesson and a different view of the legacy of Hannah Duston.

Nathanial Hawthorne, in "The Duston Family," published in *The American Magazine of Useful and Entertaining Knowledge* in 1836, has little respect for Hannah's bloody deed, focusing instead on the nobility of Thomas Duston, who was unable to choose which of his children to save: "Goodman Duston looked at the poor things, one by one; and with yearning fondness, he looked at them all, together; then he gazed up to Heaven for a moment, and finally waved his hand to his seven beloved ones. 'Go on, my children,' said he, calmly. 'We will live or die together!'"

Hawthorne closes with: "This awful woman, and that tender hearted, yet valiant man, her husband, will be remembered as long as the deeds of old times are told round a New England fireside. But how different is her renown from his!"

Henry David Thoreau, in *A Week on the Concord and Merrimack Rivers*, in 1868, recounts the tale of Hannah "Dustan," concluding by mysteriously equating Hannah's deeds with original sin:

> *According to the historian, they escaped as by a miracle all roving bands of Indians, and reached their homes in safety, with their trophies, for which the General Court paid them fifty pounds. The family of Hannah Dustan all assembled alive once more, except the infant whose brains were dashed out against the appletree, and there have been many who in later times have lived to say that they had eaten of the fruit of that appletree.*

Haverhill's own John Greenleaf Whittier, in *Legends of New England*, 1831, takes a more balanced approach, viewing the story with a combination of "admiration and horror":

Such is the simple and unvarnished story of a New England woman. The curious historian, who may hereafter search among the dim records of our "twilight time"—who may gather from the uncertain responses of tradition, the wonderful history of the past—will find much, of the similar character, to call forth by turns, admiration and horror. And the time is coming, when all these traditions shall be treasured up as a sacred legacy— when the tale of the Indian inroad and the perils of the hunter—of the sublime courage and the dark superstitions of our ancestors, will be listened to with an interest unknown to the present generation,—and those who are to fill our places will pause hereafter by the Indian's burial place, and on the site of the old battle-field, or the thrown-down garrison, with a feeling of awe and reverence, as if communing, face to face, with the spirits of that stern race, which has passed away forever.

HANNAH BRADLEY

A footnote to the story of Hannah Duston is the story of Hannah Bradley. She was among the captives who proceeded on when Hannah Duston and Mary Neff were left on the island. Somewhere along the way, Hannah Bradley was able to escape and returned home to Haverhill. Six years later, in 1703, Mrs. Bradley was captured again, and this time she was taken all the way to Montreal. She was pregnant when captured, and during the trip, she gave birth. Mrs. Bradley later said that when the baby cried, her captors would put hot embers in the infant's mouth. They told her they would allow it to live only if she let them baptize it in their manner, which entailed cutting its forehead with a knife. Later, they killed the baby anyway by piking it on a pole.

When they reached French Canada, Hannah Bradley was sold as a servant for eighty livres. When her husband heard she had been sold to the French, he traveled on foot to Montreal, found his wife and bought her back. They came back by boat from Montreal to Boston and then returned to Haverhill.

In 1706, the Indians attacked the Bradley house again. Mrs. Bradley believed that they had come purposely for her and told her husband she would rather be killed than be taken again. This time, though, everyone in the house able to lift a gun was armed against the attack. Mrs. Bradley herself killed an Indian by throwing boiling soap on him as he tried to open the gate of the garrison. He was their leader, and the rest of the attackers retreated when they saw him fall.

JOHN ADAMS FOR THE DEFENSE

BOXFORD, 1769

In the latter part of May 1769, in the town of Boxford, young Ruth Perley Ames (also spelled Eames) gave birth to a child, and on June 5, a neighbor, Mrs. Kimball, came to pay a call and to check on the health of the young mother. She was met at the door by Ruth's mother-in-law, Elizabeth Ames, who told Mrs. Kimball she could not come in because Ruth was very ill. She had vomited and purged so much that it was disagreeable to enter the chamber. Mrs. Kimball would not be dissuaded; Ruth's health was precisely the reason for her call, and she would see the invalid regardless of the condition of the room. She entered the house and went straight to the sickroom. She found the chamber to be clean, with no sign of vomiting or purging, but Ruth was lying in agony, with froth or phlegm exuding from her mouth, and she appeared to be on her deathbed. Elizabeth Ames said that Ruth had taken sick around seven o'clock that morning. Mrs. Kimball stayed by her bedside and gave what comfort she could, but by noon, Ruth was dead.

Elizabeth said she knew Ruth would die; she had the same disorder that had killed a certain Mrs. Chandler some years earlier. It was "as mortal as the plague," she said, and predicted that the baby would soon die as well.

The funeral for Ruth Perley Ames was held soon after, and none of the neighbors was invited. Instead of their local pastor, Reverend John Cushing, who was also their nearest neighbor, the service was performed by a clergyman from a neighboring town.

Mrs. Kimball was suspicious. The symptoms she had seen that day seemed to her more like those of poisoning than disease. She also found the

The ordeal of touch.
By Tom Wilhelm.

attitude of Elizabeth Ames shocking and believed she knew more than she was telling about the cause of death. As she voiced her opinion around town, others grew suspicious as well until a complaint signed by twenty-nine men, including relatives of the deceased, was preferred to the three coroners of Boxford, Henry Ingalls, Moses Dole and Abraham Choate. The coroners agreed to exhume the body of Ruth Ames to see if there was evidence to charge her mother-in-law with murder.

In 1769, the town of Boxford was a model of eighteenth-century progress. While most residents were still farmers, other professions were on the rise—builders, tailors, innkeepers and merchants prospered in Boxford. The town now had six mills and a potash manufactory, producing potash for soap and fertilizer. Boxford had at least one school in operation and had plans for four more. There were two churches in town, and though both were Congregational (Puritan), one had opened its doors to itinerant preachers with new ideas. But in matters of criminal justice, Boxford still had one foot in the past, calling on magic and superstition when hard evidence failed. The fate of Elizabeth Ames, accused of murder, would have rested on an ancient ritual called the "ordeal by touch" had it not been for an obstinate young attorney—and future president of the United States—named John Adams.

The coroners summoned a jury of twenty-five men, including thirteen physicians. Four more physicians were hired to perform the autopsy. On July 10, more than a month after the body had been buried, an inquest was opened at the meetinghouse. The inquest was attended by "a promiscuous multitude of people" that followed the coroners to the cemetery to observe the work of exhuming the body. The crowd surged around the grave so eagerly that work could not proceed until they agreed to pull back, placated by a promise that everyone would have an opportunity to look at the remains.

The body was taken to the meetinghouse, and there an autopsy was performed. Two days later, the coroner's jury made its report as follows:

> *Essex Ss.*
>
> *An Inquistion. Indented & taken at Boxford within the sd County of Essex, the Twelfth Day of July, in the Nineth year of our Sovereign Lord George, the third, by ye Grace of God, of Great Britain, France and Ireland, King, defender of ye Faith, &c, before Henry Ingalls, Moses, Dole, & Abraham Choate, Gentlemen, Coroners for our Sd. Lord the King, within the County of Essex aforesd upon the view of the Body of Ruth Eams Wife of Jona. Ames Jur. Then and there being Dead by the Oaths of Joseph Osgood,… Good and lawful Men of the County of Essex aforesd, who begin Charged and Sworn to enquire for our Lord the King, when, by what means, and how, the sd. Ruth Eames came to her Death, upon their Oaths do say, the sd. Ruth Eames on the fifth Day of June last in the morning Died of Felony (that is to say by Poison) given to her by a Person or Persons to us unknown which murder is against the peace of our sd. Lord the King, his Crown and Dignity. In Witness whereof We the sd. Coroners, as well as the sd. Jurors to this Inquisition have interchangeably put our Hands and Seals the day and year abovesaid.*

The coroner's jury was satisfied that Ruth Ames had been poisoned, but there was not sufficient evidence to link either her husband or his mother to the murder. The jury called Jonathan and Elizabeth Ames to the meetinghouse and demanded that they perform the ordeal of touch. Also known as bier right, the ordeal of touch was an ancient test of guilt or innocence based on the belief that if a murderer touches the corpse of his victim, blood will rise through the skin of the corpse. The body is laid on a table covered only by a sheet of the purest white. The accused touches the neck of the deceased with the index finger of the left hand. When a guilty hand touches the body, blood will issue, plainly visible on the white sheet, "pleading trumpet-tongued against the deep-damnation of her taking off." The ordeal of touch was a relic of the superstitions of Europe, rare but not unknown in the colonies. It had been used in the town of Woburn, Massachusetts, in Middlesex County, and it was known to be used in the colony of Virginia and in New York State as late as 1824.

Elizabeth Ames hired an up-and-coming attorney, John Adams, from Middlesex County. Adams called the ordeal of touch "nothing but black-arts and witchcraft," and with his support the Ameses refused to submit. Refusing the test gave the jury "great occasion to conclude that they were concerned in the poisoning." Elizabeth was indicted as the principal defendant in the murder of Ruth Ames, and Jonathan was charged as an accessory in the crime.

Boxford, named after the town of Boxford, England, was originally called Rowley Village, a section of the town of Rowley, which in turn had been carved out of Ipswich. Completely surrounded by other towns, Boxford managed to avoid any direct confrontations during the Indian wars. However, it was not able to avoid the witch trials.

Rebecca Blake, who married an early Boxford settler named Robert Ames, had a reputation as a "loose character" and at one point was charged with adultery. In 1692, when all sins led to witchcraft, she was cried out as a witch by other confessed witches. Under interrogation, Rebecca said yes, she had been a witch for twenty-six years, after smudging a black fingerprint in the devil's book because he promised to conceal her adultery. Rebecca Ames was convicted of witchcraft and sentenced, along with fourteen others, to be hanged on September 22, 1692. Seven of the confessed witches, including Rebecca Ames, were granted reprieves, and after seven months in prison, Rebecca was released.

The Ames family had very little money in 1692, but over the course of the next seventy-seven years, they became wealthy landowners. Rebecca's grandson was Jonathon Ames, who owned a farm in the west parish of Boxford. In June 1769, Jonathan's wife and son were imprisoned in the same Salem jail where Rebecca Ames had been held on charges of witchcraft.

Ruth Perley's family was from Linebrook parish, a sparsely populated section of Ipswich. Though not as wealthy as the Ames family, the Perley family was old and well regarded. Ruth's older brother Samuel was pastor of the church in Seabrook, New Hampshire. Twenty-one-year-old Ruth Perley, pretty and refined, caught the eye of young Jonathan Ames, and on December 19, 1768, the two were married by her brother.

Jonathan took his new bride to live at his parents' farm, but for some reason, Elizabeth never warmed up to her daughter-in-law. Maybe there was lingering resentment over the fact that there had been Perleys among the accusers in the Salem witch trials. Or perhaps it was because Ruth was already four months pregnant when she and Jonathan were married. Whatever the reason, Elizabeth Ames took a strong disliking to the new bride, and by the time of the birth, she would publicly refer to Ruth as her son's housekeeper.

Though it was impossible to link Jonathan and Elizabeth directly to the crime, circumstantial evidence against them was strong, and many people in Boxford knew of the animosity between Elizabeth Ames and her daughter-in-law. Events in the Salem jail brought even more suspicion. Mrs. Ames was heard to mutter in her sleep, "Don't tell on me Jonathan; if you do I shall be hanged." But while awake, she told the magistrates that she now believed Ruth had been poisoned and that her son had done it. She asked if she could turn King's evidence. This was too much for Jonathan, who then asked if he could turn King's evidence against his mother. Elizabeth had been the principal defendant, and Jonathan could supply more detail, so the prosecutor accepted his offer. The murder prosecution would now focus exclusively on Elizabeth Ames.

The trial would be held at the old courthouse on what is now Washington Street in Salem. John Adams was quite familiar with Salem; his wife, Abigail, had a sister who lived there, and John had argued cases in the Salem courthouse before. The prosecution would be handled by Jonathan Sewell, the Massachusetts attorney general and, at the time, a close friend of John Adams. But this would be no pleasant reunion; with public sentiment so

John Adams. *Wikimedia Commons*.

strongly against his client and even her own son lined up to testify against her, Adams would be entering the trial as the underdog.

On Tuesday, November 14, the trial opened before the Superior Court, which consisted of four judges and a jury of men from towns throughout Essex County. The doors of the courthouse opened at 8:00 a.m.; the jury was empaneled, and the charge was read. It was presented that Elizabeth Ames on the fourth day of June last, "not having the fear of God in her heart, but feloniously, wickedly and of malice aforethought intending and contriving with Poison to kill and murder one Ruth Eames, then and there being in the peace of God, and of the said Lord the King, did then & there with force and arms feloniously willfully and with of her malice aforethought, mix and mingle a great quantity of white arsenic" in the food she served to Ruth Ames. Elizabeth Ames entered a plea of not guilty. The jury was sworn in, and the first witness was called at 9:00 a.m.

The prosecution introduced dozens of witnesses against Mrs. Ames, mostly from Boxford, but others came from Ipswich, Andover, Salem and Newburyport. The most damaging testimony came from the autopsy physicians and from Mrs. Ames's son, Jonathan. Jonathan testified that five days before the death of his wife, his mother had told him that she would deprive him of his "housekeeper" by giving her a portion of ratsbane (poison used to kill rats). The night before the murder, he saw his mother give his wife a piece of bread and butter with ratsbane on in it, "as near as he could tell." He cautioned his wife against eating it.

A trial in the eighteenth century, even a high-profile murder trial, would not be expected to last more than one day. As dusk fell over Salem that November evening, the Ames trial was far from over. Candles were lighted in the old courtroom, and testimony proceeded late into the night. It was after midnight when the closing arguments began; John Adams for the defense spoke first.

In the crowded but hushed courtroom, with the flickering candlelight adding to the drama, Adams summed up his defense of Mrs. Ames. Looking only at the testimony given in court, he said, it did not appear that Mrs. Ames had been guilty of any ill behavior toward her daughter-in-law. Further, drawing on testimony from physicians called by the defense, he said it was improbable, if not impossible, for arsenic to lie so long in the body—from the evening until seven o'clock the next morning—before taking effect. In addition, had Ruth Ames been poisoned, her body would have been more putrefied when disinterred.

Concerning the testimony of Jonathan Ames, Adams said, he had shown himself to be a liar, and consequently, nothing he said could be trusted.

Ames had first said to the coroners, under oath, that he had no knowledge of anyone poisoning his wife. Now, to clear himself, he was so base as to give testimony that not only rendered him guilty of perjury but showed a direct tendency toward taking the life of his mother.

In summing up the case for the prosecution, Jonathan Sewell said it was the hearty meal Ruth Ames had eaten, which included a plate of shad in addition to the bread and butter, that had caused the delayed reaction to the poison. Or perhaps the white powder Jonathan had seen his mother put on the bread had been salt, not poison—a subterfuge intended to make discovery more difficult and confusing when she administered the true poison the next morning. As far as the body not being putrefied as much as expected, it was the opinion of the prosecution's physicians that the dose had been so large as to kill the deceased before having time to enter the bloodstream. Jonathan Ames, said Mr. Sewell, was a legal witness, and it could not be supposed that he would come to court and, in the most solemn manner, swear to that which he knows is false when that testimony would, almost certainly, take away the life of the woman who bore him.

The four judges then gave their opinions. Three judges agreed that the testimony amounted to "a violent presumption" of the defendant's guilt. The fourth was not so clear in his opinion, believing that doubt might arise from the physicians' testimony. Then, at 2:00 a.m., the case was given to the jury.

At 9:00 a.m., the court was back in session, and the prisoner was placed at the bar. The jury came in and rendered their verdict: not guilty. Elizabeth Ames was immediately released.

John Adams's success in the Ames trial was overshadowed by that of his controversial defense, a year later, of the eight British soldiers accused of murder in what became known as the Boston Massacre. His defense was that it could not be determined which of the soldiers fired the fatal shots, stating, "Facts are stubborn things; and whatever may be our wishes, our inclinations, or the dictates of our passion, they cannot alter the state of facts and evidence." It was a proposition that applied to the case of Elizabeth Ames as well.

Adams's law career was cut short by his attendance to the political needs of the American Revolution. Following the success of that endeavor, he became the second president of the United States.

In the spring of 1770, Jonathan Ames Sr. sold the farm in Boxford and moved away. The true circumstances surrounding the death of Ruth Perley Ames have never been determined.

PIRATES OF
ESSEX COUNTY
1657–1789

Essex County is known for its rocky coast and fine natural harbors. The first settlers landed on Cape Ann, at what would later be called Gloucester, in 1623, just three years after the pilgrims landed in Plymouth. In 1626, Salem was founded—a harbor town older than Boston. For the people living on the coast, the ocean had always been their livelihood. The American navy was born in Marblehead, and the privateers of Salem and Newburyport were enormously successful at disrupting British supply lines during the American Revolution.

Fishing, shipbuilding and international trade brought wealth to the towns on the coast of Essex County, but in the seventeenth and eighteenth centuries, where there was ocean commerce there were pirates. The towns of Saugus, Marblehead, Gloucester, Essex and Newburyport all knew the scourge of piracy, and pirate stories abound on the Essex coast.

Thomas Veal

In the twilight one day in 1657, so the legend goes, a small bark, or square-rigged sailing ship, painted black and flying no flag, dropped anchor near the mouth of the Saugus River. A rowboat was lowered over the side, and four men rowed up the river, where they disembarked and hiked into the

Rachel Wall. *By Tom Wilhelm.*

woods. These movements were observed by the residents of the coast, who owed their survival to constant vigilance. The information spread from house to house, as everyone shared speculations on the nature of the strangers' business. The next morning all eyes turned to the shore to get a better look at the strange vessel, but it had sailed away in the night. There was no trace of the rowboat or the four men who had come ashore.

At the time, Saugus, which was still part of Lynn, was the site of a huge ironworks employing more than one hundred men. A workman on his way to the forge that morning found a paper left on the road where it would be easily seen. The unsigned message said that if a certain quantity of shackles, handcuffs and other iron tools were manufactured and secretly left at a specified spot in the woods, an amount of silver, equal to their value, would be found there the next day. The shackles and other articles were made, and the directions for their delivery were followed to the letter. That night, though a strict watch was kept on the coast, there was no sign of a vessel, but the following morning, the goods were gone and the promised amount of silver had been left in their place.

Some months later, the four men returned and took up residence in the woods near Saugus. They were pirates who had come to retire or at least take a respite from their life of crime. The captain, Thomas Veal (sometimes spelled Veale), had brought a pale and beautiful woman with him. The spot they picked was deep in the woods but near a cliff from which they had an expansive view of the sea to the south and much of the surrounding land—a site perfectly suited to concealment and observation. They built a small hut, planted a garden and dug a well.

The pirates' peaceful retreat did not last long. Gossip of the pirates' glen spread through the colony, and before long, British soldiers came to investigate. Three of the pirates were captured and taken back to England, where they were very likely hanged. The beautiful woman had taken sick and died; she was buried in an unmarked grave in the woods. The only one left was their leader, Thomas Veal, who had managed to escape capture.

Veal took up residence in a cavern in the woods where he and his comrades had hidden their ill-gotten treasure. He practiced the trade of shoemaking and would occasionally come into town to trade for food and supplies but otherwise lived in seclusion.

In 1658, New England experienced a great earthquake. This devastating event was recorded by Secretary Nathaniel Morton of the Plymouth Colony and by other commentators at the time. The movement of the earth split the foundations of the cavern and sealed the entrance, trapping Thomas Veal and his gold forever. Since then, the cliff has been known as Dungeon Rock, and the former home of the pirates is known as the Pirates' Glen.

In the 1830s, there were two attempts to blast open Dungeon Rock, retrieve the remains of Thomas Veal and recover his treasure; both failed. Thomas Veal and his buried treasure fired imaginations for generations, and for some, dreams of gold became an obsession. In 1852, Hiram Marble built a house near Dungeon Rock and began excavating. He moved his family to the house, and Hiram and his son Edwin dug together through the rock until Hiram's death in 1868. Edwin continued the work until his own death in 1880. They never reached the treasure.

Hiram Marble was a member of the Spiritualist Church and claimed that he had received a message from Thomas Veal telling him that if he came to dig

Dungeon Rock, Lynn Woods. *Photo by Peter Meo.*

at Dungeon Rock he would leave a rich man. But Marble was not motivated by simple greed; his true wish was to prove that it was possible to communicate with the dead, and he planned to use the treasure to buy the site and preserve it as a public park. Though Marble did not prove the existence of the spirit world, shortly after his son's death, the City of Lynn did purchase the land around Dungeon Rock to include in its new park, Lynn Woods.

JOHN PHILIPS

On April 14, 1724, the sloop *Squirrel*, skippered by Andrew Haraden, set sail from Annisquam Harbor (now part of Gloucester) on a fishing voyage. The *Squirrel* was newly built—in fact, the deck work had not been completed—but the owner and the captain were both anxious to take out the new sloop. It was proposed that the work be finished during the voyage, so all of the necessary tools—including an adz and a broadaxe—had been brought along.

As they moved into Ipswich Bay, Captain Haraden noticed another ship following roughly the same course as the *Squirrel*. By the time they reached the Isles of Shoals off the New Hampshire coast, the other ship was still with them and had moved even closer. Then Haraden saw a puff of smoke from

Annisquam. *Photo by Peter Meo.*

a swivel gun on the rail of the other ship, and a moment later, a cannonball struck the water fewer than one hundred feet off the *Squirrel*'s bow. The firing ship then hoisted a black flag and commanded the captain of the *Squirrel* to row across to their ship. The *Squirrel* was not armed, and Captain Haraden had no choice but to comply.

When he reached the other ship, he learned the identity of his assailant. It was the pirate Captain John Phillips, who had taken several fishing vessels off Cape Ann the year before. He had spent the winter in the West Indies and was bringing his ship, the *Revenge*, north, making captures on the American coast as he went.

Even in pirate circles, John Phillips was not highly regarded. His ship was small, and he had a crew of fewer than twenty men, some of whom had been captured and forced into service. In fact, that is how Phillips himself became a pirate; he was a carpenter traveling from England to Newfoundland when his ship was taken by the pirate Captain Antsis in the ship *Good Fortune*. Phillips soon reconciled himself to the life of a pirate and joined the crew on the violent capture of at least one other ship on the way to Tobago in the West Indies.

When they reached the Indies, the crew of the *Good Fortune* broke up. Some wanted to continue sailing under the black flag, and others wanted to

Pirate Captain John Phillips forcing a prisoner at gunpoint to drink alcohol. *Wikimedia Commons.*

petition the King for a pardon. The petition was drawn up and signed, and several crew members, including Phillips, traveled to England to deliver it. The pardon was not granted, and when he learned that some of the crew had been arrested, Phillips shipped out again for Newfoundland. There he deserted and for a season took a job as a fish splitter. In Boston, he convinced sixteen of his coworkers to join him in stealing a schooner and returning to piracy. Only four showed up, but they decided to proceed anyway, planning to enlarge the company as they went. They stole a schooner, renamed it the *Revenge* and drew up articles of piracy—one of the few surviving complete articles of piracy:

> *I. Every Man Shall obey civil Command; the Captain shall have one full Share and a half of all Prizes; the Master, Carpenter, Boatswain and Gunner shall have one Share and quarter.*
> *II. If any Man shall offer to run away, or keep any Secret from the Company, he shall be marooned with one Bottle of Powder, one Bottle of Water, one small Arm, and Shot.*
> *III. If any Man shall steal any Thing in the Company, or game, to the Value of a Piece of Eight, he shall be marooned or shot.*
> *IV. If any time we shall meet another Marooner that Man shall sign his Articles without the Consent of our Company, shall suffer such Punishment as the Captain and Company shall think fit.*

V. That Man that shall strike another whilst these Articles are in force, shall receive Moses's Law (that is, 40 Stripes lacking one) on the bare Back.

VI. That Man that shall snap his Arms, or smoke Tobacco in the Hold, without a Cap to his Pipe, or carry a Candle lighted without a Lanthorn, shall suffer the same Punishment as in the former Article.

VII. That Man shall not keep his Arms clean, fit for an Engagement, or neglect his Business, shall be cut off from his Share, and suffer such other Punishment as the Captain and the Company shall think fit.

VIII. If any Man shall lose a Joint in time of an Engagement, shall have 400 Pieces of Eight; if a Limb, 800.

IX. If at any time you meet with a prudent Woman, that Man that offers to meddle with her, without her Consent, shall suffer present Death.

They did not have a Bible aboard the *Revenge*, so the pirates swore their oaths on a hatchet.

When he captured the *Squirrel*, Phillips saw right away that it was a new vessel, and from the lines he could tell it was fast. He ordered his men to load all the guns, ammunition and provisions from the *Revenge* onto the *Squirrel*. Captain Haraden was taken captive, and the rest of his crew was put aboard the empty *Revenge* to fend for themselves.

The *Squirrel* had not gone far before Andrew Haraden realized that much of Phillips's crew was against him. Edward Cheeseman, a ship's carpenter, revealed to him that a number of plots to overthrow the captain had already been discussed among them. He thought the extra tools aboard the *Squirrel* could be used to their advantage. Another member of the crew, John Fillmore, was also anxious to join the plot. Fillmore was a fisherman from Wenham, not far from Annisquam, who had been captured by Phillips the previous fall. They rejected a plan to strike Phillips at night, thinking that without firearms the possibility of confusion and mistake was too great. They decided to attack at noon on April 17.

Cheeseman engaged in conversation with sailing master John Nutt, who was the greatest physical threat among the pirates, while Fillmore took the broadaxe and began whirling it around as if at play. When the signal was given, Cheeseman grabbed Nutt and threw him overboard, where he drowned. Then Fillmore swung the broadaxe at the boatswain's neck, severing his head. Captain Phillips came running to the deck, and Cheeseman broke his jaw with a mallet. Haraden went at Phillips with the adz but was prevented by Sparks, the gunner. Some other members of the conspiracy dispatched Sparks over the side, and Haraden smashed Phillips's head with the adz, killing him. They were prepared to murder John Rose Archer, the quartermaster, but seeing that they now had the upper hand, the conspirators thought it better to take him to shore and let him face justice.

Captain Haraden took command of the *Squirrel* and sailed it back to Annisquam. John Phillips had been decapitated, and as the ship entered the harbor, his head could be seen hanging from the masthead. The incident was immediately reported, and the crew of the *Revenge*—four pirates and seven forced men—was taken to Boston for trial. Two men were found guilty and sentenced to hang: John Rose Archer, who had previously sailed under Blackbeard the pirate in the Carolinas, and twenty-two-year-old William White.

They were hanged at the ferry way in Boston, leading to Charlestown, in front of a multitude of spectators. At one end of the gallows hung the pirate flag of the *Revenge*, a black flag, "in the middle of which an Anatomy, and at one side of it a Dart in the Heart, with drops of blood proceeding from it; and on the other side an Hour-glass." Their bodies were then taken to an island near Annisquam—later known as Hangman's Island—and left there to hang. Traditionally, the bodies of pirates were left hanging until completely decomposed to serve as a warning for others.

John Fillmore, the Wenham fisherman who had been instrumental in retaking the *Squirrel*, left a written account of the entire incident. He was the great-grandfather of Millard Fillmore, the thirteenth president of the United States.

Rachel Wall

The most fascinating pirate of Essex County was Rachel Wall, New England's only female pirate. She was born Rachel Schmidt in Carlisle, Pennsylvania, in 1760, and at age sixteen, she married a sailor named George Wall. The couple lived in poverty until they moved to Boston, where Rachel took a job as a maid and George worked on a fishing schooner.

After returning from a three-month fishing trip, George took Rachel out drinking with five of his fellow sailors and their lady friends. It was a binge that lasted a full week, and by the end, they had drunk up three months' pay. Rachel would say later, "He enticed me to leave my service and take to bad company, from which I date my ruin." The Walls were poor once again, and the schooner had already left on another voyage. They had to find another way to live.

George Wall and his five friends had sailed on privateers during the American Revolution. They worked on board ships that were licensed by the Massachusetts government to attack British cargo vessels and commandeer their freight. It is not a great leap from privateer to pirate, and the men decided to make use of their experience in capturing ships and become buccaneers. George Wall was to be their captain, and knowing he would need all the hands he could get, he asked his wife, Rachel, to join them.

There had been female pirates who were famous enough in 1780 for Rachel Wall to have known their histories. Mary Read and Anne Bonny, two female pirates who both fought in men's clothing, by chance both found themselves together in the crew of pirate captain Calico Jack. In 1720, they were captured in Jamaica and sentenced to hang. Both "pled the belly," claiming to be pregnant to avoid hanging. Mary died in prison, and Anne, who may have actually been pregnant, was reprieved. Pirating was clearly a dangerous venture, but Rachel Wall was game.

Rachel and the men obtained a ship in the town of Essex on Cape Ann, which at the time had a fleet of fishing vessels and had already become famous for its shipbuilding. Sources differ on whether the schooner they took was stolen or borrowed, but in either case, it is safe to say the owner did not know they intended to use it for piracy.

Between Cape Ann and the Isles of Shoals, they would take the ship out after a storm, raise a distress flag and give the appearance of being out of control. When a ship came to their aid, its sailors would see Rachel standing at the rail and would be even more anxious to help what appeared to be a storm-damaged vessel. When the rescue ship was along their side, the pirates would storm the crew and murder them all. After unloading the cargo and all valuables, they would scuttle the rescue ship, leaving the impression that it had been lost in the storm.

The plan worked well, and between 1781 and 1782, they captured at least twelve ships, netting about $6,000 worth of cash and merchandise—an estimated $110,000 in current dollars. But in September 1782, their fortunes turned. The morning after a severe storm, they went out near the Isles of Shoals to ply their trade as usual, but what they thought was a clear autumn day was probably the eye of a hurricane. They soon found themselves in the middle of a storm as ferocious as the one the day before, and now their ship was truly in distress. The winds were so strong that they snapped the mainmast, which knocked George Wall and another crewman overboard, drowning both men. The survivors, including Rachel Wall, were rescued the following day by a brig from New York. The pirates made no attempts to rob it.

Rachel went back to Boston and returned to her old job as maid, but she had become accustomed to the excitement and easy money of crime. Legend says she would sneak aboard ships in the harbor and leave with whatever she could carry. Other sources suggest that Rachel turned to prostitution and would rob her clients after they had fallen asleep. In 1789, she was arrested for robbery and suspicion of murdering a sailor who had been found dead on the waterfront.

At her trial, Rachel Wall freely confessed her acts of piracy, admitting "to have been guilty of many crimes such as Sabbath-breaking, stealing, lying, disobedience to parents, and almost any other sin a person could commit except murder." But the jury was not convinced, and Rachel was found guilty and sentenced to hang.

On October 8, 1789, Rachel Wall, along with convicted highwaymen William Smith and William Dunogan, was transported in a horse-drawn wagon from jail to Boston Common, where a large crowd had gathered to witness the execution. The wagon was a combination hangman's cart and gallows. After they reached their destination, the three prisoners were hanged from the vehicle that had delivered them. Rachel Wall's last words were: "And now, into the hands of the Almighty God, I commit my soul, and relying on his mercy, through the merits and mediations of my Redeemer, and die an unworthy member of the Presbyterian Church, in the 29th year of my life."

She was the last woman hanged in Massachusetts and the last American female pirate.

POMP
ANDOVER, 1795

Before going to bed on the night of February 11, 1795, Mrs. Sarah Furbush asked her husband, Captain Charles Furbush, if he had locked up their African slave, Pomp, for the night. Pomp was prone to fits at unpredictable times, and the family believed he was somewhat insane. For the safety of the household, Pomp's bedroom door was bolted shut from the outside on most nights. On this February night, Captain Furbush responded to his wife that Pomp had seemed well and he had decided not to bolt the door.

Sometime between the hours of ten and eleven o'clock, Pomp quietly entered his master's bedroom carrying an axe from the fireplace downstairs. In the moonlight, he distinguished which of the sleeping bodies was Captain Furbush, raised the axe and, with murderous force, swung it down on his sleeping master, striking him on the back of the head, just above the temple. Pomp struck a second blow and then quietly walked from the room.

The animosity Pomp felt toward Captain Furbush and his discontent over his current situation was well known. He had tried to run away several times and had even sought help from the selectmen of Andover. The murder could have been prevented if someone had just listened to Pomp's complaints. But what is most tragic is that Pomp should not have been forced to stay; slavery had been effectively abolished in Massachusetts fifteen years before the murder.

The institution of slavery was introduced in Massachusetts as early as the 1620s. The Puritans saw no moral problem with slavery; they cited scripture as justification and believed that Africans and Native Americans were not

Pomp

The murder of Captain Furbush. *By Tom Wilhelm.*

capable of salvation. But by the mid-1700s, sentiment in Massachusetts was turning in favor of abolition. Slavery was effectively abolished in 1780, more by legal subtlety than by proclamation. The Massachusetts Constitution, drafted by John Adams, Samuel Adams and James Bowdoin and ratified in 1780, contains the statement, "All men are born free and equal, and have certain natural, essential, and unalienable rights." Though the clause was not intended to free the slaves, it became the foundation for legal challenges to slavery. Case by case, court decisions led to an interpretation of the constitution that was incompatible with slavery. But for a time, the situation remained ambiguous, leaving African Americans in Massachusetts unsure of their legal status.

Slavery had never been as profitable in Massachusetts as it was in the South. The small farms in New England could not take advantage of multitudes of unskilled workers the way the cotton and tobacco plantations of the South could. Manufacturing was on the rise in New England, and that required training that employers were reluctant to give to slaves.

Many wealthy Essex County households, however, depended on slave labor, and in some cases, the relationships between these families and their slaves became close and long term. The Reverend Samuel Phillips, in Andover, owned several slaves, including a man named Cato who stayed with the family through seven generations and remained with them even after his freedom was possible.

But not all relations lasted so long or ran so smoothly; in 1770, advertisements like the following appeared in the *Essex Gazette*:

To be sold by the subscriber cheap for cash or Good Security, a Healthy, Strong Negro Boy, 20 years old last month, very ingenious in the farming business and can work in iron-work both at blowing and refining and as I am done with the Iron works I have more help than I need on my farm. James Frye. Andover Apr. 9, 1770

To be Sold a Likely, Healthy Negro girl about 14 years old, Enquire to MR. Thomas Bragg, Deputy Sheriff in Andover. September 8, 1770

Fugitive slave notices also appeared: "Ran away from the subscriber on the 24th day of September a Man Servant about 19 years of age, named Isaac Mott. He had on when he went away a blue serge coat and a flowered flannel jacket and leather breeches. Whosoever will take up the said runaway and bring him to me shall be rewarded. Jonathan Abbot. Andover Oct. 10 1770"

The Abbots of Andover seemed to have ongoing trouble holding on to their slaves. In 1786, David Abbot was Pomp's owner, and the sixteen-year-old slave had run away several times; each time, he was captured and returned. Pomp had an unusual history. He had come to America with his parents, who moved from Guinea, in Africa, to Boston. As unusual as it was, they may have come to America from Africa as free people. But soon after their arrival, Pomp's father died, and his mother sold him to David Abbot's father. Pomp stayed in touch with his mother and his siblings who still lived in Boston, and Boston was thought to have been his destination when Pomp bolted from Abbot's farm.

Pomp must have heard that slaves in Massachusetts had successfully sued for their freedom because he told David Abbot that he intended to leave. When Abbot replied that Pomp was not free and had to stay on Abbot's farm, Pomp went to the selectmen of Andover and asked them whether he had the right to leave. They did not give him a definitive answer but advised he stay with Abbot for a while longer. In the meantime, the selectmen arranged for Pomp to leave Abbot and go to work for Captain Charles Furbush, assuming Pomp would find Furbush a more agreeable master.

The Furbushes were an old and established Essex County family. Fifty-nine-year-old Charles Furbush was born in Andover and lived there his entire life. He was tall, strong and an excellent horseman; he was considered one of the finest judges of horseflesh of his day. As a young man, he had fought in the French and Indian War at the forts on Lake George and Lake Champlain. During the Revolutionary War, he fought at the Battle of Lexington with a group of minutemen made up of volunteers from towns throughout Essex County. He rose to become the captain of a company from Andover that was stationed in Cambridge and fought at the Battle of Bunker Hill. During the war, he met several times with General George Washington and met him again after the war when President Washington visited Andover.

Pomp went to work on Captain Furbush's farm. They worked together for a while, but Furbush turned his attention to his horses, leaving Pomp to manage the farm alone. According to Pomp's statement, he cut all of the hay and raised 170 bushels of corn a year with only the occasional help of one of Furbush's sons. He found Captain Furbush to be no better a master than Abbot had been. The captain would not allow Pomp to go to meeting on Sundays but instead made him clear out the cattle on the Sabbath. Pomp was severely flogged when his work was not to the captain's liking. Three times Pomp tried to run away from the farm; each time, he was brought back and flogged. The third time he was left naked and tied up outside on the ground overnight in the icy weather of late fall.

To complicate Pomp's problems, around the time he went to work for Captain Furbush, he began having convulsions. The fits would come on him at unpredictable times, and the Furbushes thought that Pomp was probably insane. The practice of bolting his door at night began out of fear that, in a fit of insanity, Pomp might go into the room of the captain's daughters.

In spite of Pomp's flaws, Captain Furbush told him he could stay at the house as long as he pleased and added that he would not be in the world forever. In his limited understanding of the world, Pomp took this to mean that upon his master's death, the Furbush farm and even Mrs. Furbush would belong to him. Pomp later said, "The hopes of being master, husband and owner, on one hand, and the cruel treatment I received from Furbush on the other, prompted me to wish for his death and produced an idea of hastening [it] by [killing] him myself."

The axe blows to her husband's head startled Mrs. Furbush awake. She raised him up and found there was a sound in his throat but he could not regain his breath. She ran to the room of her daughter, Martha, the only other family member in the house at the time, saying, "Pomp has killed your father." They both ran from the house. Mrs. Furbush left Martha with a neighbor and then went on to her son's house.

After they had left, Pomp went back into the bedroom, pulled the body from the bed and, for good measure, cut the throat of his victim. He then repaired to the next room, built a fire, lit all the candles he could find and sat there until the relatives arrived and locked him back in his room.

Pomp would later claim that on that night he had suffered a fit soon after going to bed. It had been so severe that he nearly bit through his tongue and was delirious coming out of it. When the fit subsided, he became obsessed with the idea of killing his master. He went to the fireplace and picked up the axe. As he passed a mirror, he was horrified by his reflection, but something kept whispering in his ear, "Now is your time! Kill him now! Now or never! Now! Now!"

Mrs. Furbush did not believe that the murder was committed on impulse but thought that it was adroitly planned and consummated. He had chosen a night when most of the family members were away on a visit. He had taken the axe and concealed himself under the stairs instead of going to his room. It would not have mattered if his door had been bolted because he was not inside. Some of the neighbors were not surprised, claiming that Pomp had told them he intended to kill his master.

Pomp was baffled by all that happened next. Instead of taking possession of his master's property, he was told he would hang. This sent him into a panic because in his experience punishment was always immediate; he would be flogged right after his crime or not at all. When he wasn't immediately hanged, he believed he was safe. Pomp was tried in Ipswich, convicted of murder and sentenced to hang.

Before his execution, Pomp was visited by several ministers who believed that his problems arose from being kept from the word of God. They taught him to pray, and after learning how, he did so ten to twenty times a day, believing in the power of prayer to improve his life. He said, "I never felt so [well] and hearty in my life as I now am, [the] fits and lunacy have left me entirely [and I] hope to behave cleverly and graciously in this world." He even believed that the intense praying had begun to lighten his skin.

Pomp was executed on August 6, 1795. He was taken to Gallowes Field, on the corner of Rowley Road and Mile Lane, where he was hanged in front of a large crowd. Before his death, Pomp was interviewed by Jonathan Plummer, one of the first professional writers in the United States. Plummer wrote a pamphlet entitled *Dying Confession of Pomp, A Negro Man, Who Was Executed at Ipswich, on the 6th August, 1795, for Murdering Capt. Charles Furbush, of Andover, Taken from the Mouth of the Prisoner, and Penned by Jonathan Plummer, Jun.* The pamphlet preserved Pomp's side of the story, though Jonathan Plummer was skeptical of his claim to being driven by voices. After his death, Pomp's skull was obtained by a physician in Georgetown, Massachusetts, and for years was used as an example in the study of phrenology, the belief that a person's character was determined by the shape of his head.

VENGEFUL FIRE

NEWBURYPORT, 1820

About half past nine o'clock on the night of May 31, 1811, people in downtown Newburyport noticed a cloud of smoke filling the sky above Inn Street. Moments later, a column of flame shot up from a stable, and the cry of "Fire!" rang through Market Square. Fanned by a westerly wind, the blaze quickly raged through the densely packed wooden structures of Newburyport. The town's six volunteer fire companies sprang into action using hand tub pump wagons to douse the flame. Two lines of people formed a bucket brigade between the Merrimack River and the fire; men passed leather buckets, filled with water, to the front, while women and children passed the empty buckets back to the river. But the effort was hopelessly inadequate, as the fire consumed businesses and homes, growing ever larger until at one point, the flames from both sides of State Street converged in an arc above the road.

The glow of the fire could be seen by all the towns surrounding Newburyport and as far north as Amherst, New Hampshire. The neighboring towns sent what help they could, but it was futile; by two o'clock that morning, the whole town of Newburyport seemed destined for destruction. The men of the town started tearing down buildings in the fire's path in hope of stopping its forward motion. Then, mercifully, about four o'clock that morning, the wind shifted, reversing direction, and the fire, pushed back on its path of destruction, had nothing left to consume.

The morning light revealed the extent of the devastation. Sixteen and a half acres of the most densely packed section of Newburyport had been

Vengeful fire. *By Tom Wilhelm.*

completely destroyed. About 250 buildings—90 homes, the rest stores and businesses—were burned to the ground. The damage amounted to $1 million, a staggering sum in 1811. The residents of Newburyport opened their homes to those who had been left homeless by the fire. Financial aid came from the city of Salem and the towns of Essex County, from Boston and from as far away as Philadelphia. Shakers from New Hampshire delivered five cartloads of furniture, food and clothing. The town was eternally grateful, and once back on their feet, Newburyporters became famous for their support for other communities in their hour of need.

Arson was suspected as the cause of the fire. There had been several other fires that spring, quickly contained but unexplained. There was no hard evidence of arson, and no one was ever accused, but the fear remained.

The State of Massachusetts enacted regulations requiring buildings between Market Square and Federal Street to be made of brick or stone. No wooden structure in town could be taller than twenty-five feet, and firewalls were required to be built between buildings. Reconstruction was hindered by economic hardships brought on by the War of 1812, but once it was finished, many commented that the town looked better than ever.

Nine years later, Newburyport once again experienced the terror of unexplained fires. On May 18, 1820, a hay-filled barn on Green Street burned to the ground. Another barn caught fire on August 16. Then, on the morning of August 17, just before daylight, a fire started in a barn belonging to Mrs. Phoebe Cross on Temple Street. Four homes adjacent to the barn burned to the ground, along with six other buildings. This time the people of Newburyport had no doubt that the cause was arson, and the prime suspect was a sixteen-year-old boy named Stephen Merrill Clark.

Stephen Clark was a troubled child, prone to bad behavior that was often too much for his father, Moses Clark, to handle. As he grew up, Stephen was known for profanity, habitual lying and vulgar insolence to his superiors. At age thirteen, he was apprenticed to his brother to learn the trade of baking but was soon sent away for bad conduct. He was then apprenticed to a cooper but was dismissed by his master after three weeks for gross misconduct and theft. At fourteen, he was brought before the magistrate for assault and battery on an old man.

In 1820, Stephen Clark seemed to harbor a grudge against all of Newburyport. He was having a relationship with a woman named Hannah Downes, who was politely referred to as "an abandoned woman." Stephen bitterly resented the way Hannah was treated by his family and the people of Newburyport and was very vocal in his resentment. When it looked as though Stephen was about to be arrested for arson, his father sent him to the town of Belfast, Maine. Before he left, Stephen told Hannah Downes that he planned to return to Newburyport and set more fires.

Hannah Downes was a prostitute working at a brothel run by Mrs. Sally Chase, and her relationship with Stephen Clark had been well known. When the magistrates learned that Clark had left town, both Hannah and Mrs. Chase were arrested as "lewd and lascivious characters." Hannah was released after a week, but Sally Chase was held for a month, after which she changed her ways and became a servant for Mr. Wade, the keeper of the prison.

Mrs. Chase recognized Stephen Clark when he returned to Newburyport on September 22, and she told her employer he was back in town. Mr. Wade grabbed Stephen and took him to the magistrate, who arrested Stephen for arson. Hannah Downes had also been arrested again, and though they were separated by a stone wall, she and Stephen were in adjacent jail cells. Stephen managed to get a note to Hannah telling her to keep silent, but she was no longer on his side. She told the magistrate everything she knew about Stephen's involvement in the fire and his plans to set more fires. When confronted with the detailed evidence provided by Hannah Downes, Stephen confessed.

On February 15, 1821, the trial of Stephen Merrill Clark for arson commenced before the supreme judicial court in Salem. Arson, at the time, was a capital offense, and Clark would be fighting for his life. He now pled not guilty, claiming the confession had been coerced through threat of punishment if he failed to confess and promise of reward if he did confess.

Stone jail in Newburyport, built in the 1820s. *Photo by Peter Meo.*

Moses Clark provided an alibi for his son, claiming that Stephen had been at home the whole night of the fire.

The primary witnesses against Clark were Hannah Downes and Sally Chase. Hannah testified that he was with them the morning after the fire. She told the court that Clark observed that night that "the fire blazed damned well, and the fellow who made it was a damned good fellow—and if he knew him he would treat him." Hannah replied to Clark that she believed he knew as much about the matter as anyone, to which Stephen nodded assent.

He later confessed the whole thing to her. He said he had gone to his father's cellar for a candle, and after breaking it accidentally, he thought it could serve another purpose. He took the candle, some matches and a lighted cigar and climbed to the upper loft of Mrs. Cross's barn. He stuck the candle upright in a pile of hay and then lit it using the cigar and matches. This took place around eight or nine o'clock; he went back home and went to bed so he would not be suspected. Around midnight, he awoke and, since he hadn't heard an alarm, thought the candle had gone out. At two o'clock, he woke again and saw that the fire had started and his plan had worked. Hannah further testified that Clark had told her he planned to return to Newburyport and start fires at four different locations so that as people tried to extinguish one, another would break out somewhere else. Mrs. Chase confirmed what Hannah Downes had said and added that while Clark was free, the town was in imminent danger. She said, "I told him to take care what he said; he said he did not care a God damn; he would have his revenge on Newburyport; he would have his revenge on his brother for opposing his going with Hannah Downes."

Stephen Clark's attorney, a public defender, challenged the methods used to extract a confession from Clark and presented testimony to back up his alibi. He also did all he could to discredit the testimony of the two witnesses whom he called "night-walkers" and "persons of lascivious behavior," "on whose word no reliance can be placed." Moses Clark testified that prior to the fire he had gone to see Hannah Downes and said he did not know what she meant by enticing his son unless it was to undo him. She replied that she did mean to undo him. He sent his son to Belfast not to escape justice but to keep him from these girls who meant to ruin him.

The case was given to the jury at half past four o'clock in the afternoon. At nine o'clock that evening, they returned a verdict of guilty. Members of the jury, none of whom was from Newburyport, unanimously appealed for a commutation of the sentence from execution to prison time. The appeal was denied, and Stephen Merrill Clark was sentenced to hang.

In the interval between the sentencing and the date of his execution, there was a strenuous effort to spare the life of sixteen-year-old Stephen Clark. A petition signed by many of the most respectable people in Essex County was presented to the governor. Newspapers throughout the county published letters, some supporting and some condemning the hanging. The governor, citing "regard to the safety of the community," refused to commute the sentence.

The day before the execution, Clark expressed a desire to make a complete confession. A number of questions were prepared, and in the presence of four or five witnesses, he gave his answers. He said he had been induced to set fire to Newburyport as revenge for what people had said about his relationship with Hannah. The talk had deeply offended her, and she urged him to commit the act. At first he did not want to do it, but she talked him into it.

On May 10, 1821, a crowd of more than ten thousand people turned out to see the execution of Stephen Merrill Clark on Winter Island in Salem Harbor. Newspapers at the time reported that Clark approached the gallows with a resigned, contrite demeanor, but in 1837, a legislative committee debating the abolition of the death penalty heard a different story: "Such was his horror of death that it was found necessary, amidst his cries and lamentations, actually to force him from his cell, and drag him to the place of execution."

At two o'clock in the afternoon, sixteen-year-old Stephen Clark was "launched into eternity"; he died quickly without apparent suffering.

"A MOST EXTRAORDINARY CASE"

SALEM, 1830

In the years leading up to the American Revolution, the city of Salem had grown to be a busy seaport and a major mercantile center for the colonies. When war broke out and the harbors of Boston and New York were occupied by the British, the colonies turned to Salem for maritime help. The merchants of Salem had passed a resolution in town meeting on June 12, 1776, that "if the Honorable Congress shall for the Safety of the United American Colonies declare them Independent of the Kingdom of Great Britain, we will solemnly engage, with our lives and fortunes, to support them in measure."

True to their word, they turned their merchant vessels into men of war and built new ones, equipped with cannons and manned with sailors, and sent them out to fight the greatest sea power on earth. Salem sent out at least 158 privateers, with twelve to fourteen cannons each. They captured as many as 445 British ships.

When the war ended, the merchants of Salem found themselves in possession of many large, swift-sailing vessels, newly built for privateering. These ships were ideal for world trade, and Salem ships began traveling to seaports throughout Europe and Asia. They returned with sugar, coffee, rum and spices of all kinds. The shops on Derby Street were filled with strange and unique articles from distant lands, including parrots, monkeys and other exotic animals. Salem became a principal distribution point for

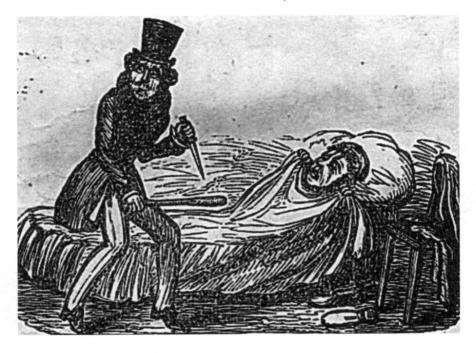

Above: *From* Trial of John Francis Knapp for the Murder of Capt. Joseph White of Salem.

Right: *Joseph White*, by Benjamin Blyth. *Courtesy of Peabody Essex Museum.*

foreign merchandise; in 1800 alone, eight million pounds of sugar passed through Salem Harbor.

Captain Joseph White was one of the traders who made his fortune on the Salem merchant fleet. In 1830, at age eighty-two, he had retired and was living comfortably in his Essex Street mansion—an old Federal-style home he had purchased sixteen years earlier. Captain White had never married, and at the time he was sharing his home with his niece, Mrs. Mary Beckford, who served as housekeeper. He also employed a live-in maid and a manservant.

On April 5, 1830, Mrs. Beckford went to Wenham to spend a few days with Mr. and Mrs. Joseph Knapp Jr., her daughter and son-in-law. Mr. Knapp's father, Joseph Knapp Sr., had been the captain of a ship owned by Joseph White. The morning of April 7, Captain White's servant noticed that the back window of the parlor was open and a plank had been raised to the window from the backyard. He informed the maid, and the two proceeded to inspect the house for any signs of theft. They found nothing amiss until they came to Captain White's bedroom. The bedroom door was ajar, and when they entered the room, they were horrified to find the captain lying stiffly in bed with the sheets turned down and his nightclothes saturated in blood. They immediately sent for the authorities, who examined the body closely and found that his skull had been fractured by a blow that had not broken the skin and his body had been stabbed thirteen times with a long dagger.

The motive for the crime was a mystery. Nothing had been stolen, and Captain White had been an amiable old man with no enemies. The parlor window, which was usually locked from the inside, had been left unlatched that night. The servants were suspected at first, but footprints found in the garden by the plank matched neither of their shoes. Besides, they were old and trusted employees who had no reason to kill their master. Then there was the matter of Captain White's niece, Mrs. Beckford, who slept in the room closest to his and was conveniently absent that night.

The incident threw the city into a state of alarm. On the day of Captain White's funeral, business in Salem was almost completely suspended. Rewards were offered for the apprehension of the killer, and a Committee of Vigilance was appointed to investigate the matter.

On April 27, with the town still in a state of heightened excitement, Joseph Knapp Jr. and his brother John Francis Knapp (known as Frank) went before the Committee of Vigilance and testified that on the preceding evening, while returning in a chaise—a two-wheeled carriage—from Salem to their home in Wenham, they were attacked by a band of robbers as they passed Wenham Pond. One grabbed the horse's bridle, while the other two seized a small trunk in the bottom of the chaise. The brothers resisted, but the robbers took their plunder and disappeared into the darkness. This statement caused many to believe that a gang of assassins was operating in Essex County, and although nothing had been stolen from Captain White, it was believed that this gang was responsible for his murder.

Weeks passed, and no progress was made in solving the mystery of the murder or in apprehending the alleged gang of assassins. Then a rumor began to circulate in the jail in New Bedford, seventy miles south of Salem. A prisoner named Hatch, who had been arrested for shoplifting before the murder, intimated that he could supply some information. Under interrogation, he stated that some months before the murder, and before his arrest, he had been an associate of Richard Crowninshield, a machinist who had a bad reputation in Salem and Danvers. He had often heard Crowninshield express his intention of killing Captain White. Hatch was taken before the grand jury, and an indictment was issued against Crowninshield. On May 2, Richard Crowninshield, his brother George and two other men who had been seen with them in a Salem gambling house the night of the murder were arrested. The Crowninshield brothers were held, and the other two were released.

On May 12, Joseph J. Knapp Sr. received the following letter:

Belfast, May 12, 1830.

Dear Sir:—I have taken the pen at this time to address an utter stranger, and strange as it may seem to you, it is for the purpose of requesting the loan of three hundred and fifty dollars, for which I can give you no security but my word, and in this case consider this to be sufficient. My call for money at this time is pressing, or I would not trouble you; but with that sum, I have the prospect of turning it to so much advantage, as to be able to refund it with interest in the course of six months. At all events, I think it will be for your interest to comply with my request, and that immediately—that is, not to put off any longer than you receive this. Then set down and inclose me the money with as much despatch as possible, for your own interest. This, Sir, is my advice; and if you do not comply with it, the short period between now and November will convince you that you have denied a request, the granting of which will never injure you, the refusal of which will ruin you. Are you surprised at this assertion?—rest assured that I make it reserving to myself the reasons and a series of facts which are founded on such a bottom as will bid defiance to property or quality. It is useless for me to enter into a discussion of facts which must inevitably harrow up your soul. No, I will merely tell you that I am acquainted with your brother Frank, and also the business that he was transacting for you on the 2ⁿᵈ of April last; and that I think that you was very extravagant in giving one thousand dollars to the person that would execute the business for you. But you know best about that, you see that such things will leak out. To conclude, Sir, I will inform you that there is a gentleman of my acquaintance in Salem that will observe that you do not leave town before the first of June, giving you sufficient time between now and then to comply with my request; and if I do not receive a line from you, together with the above sum, before the 22d of this month. I shall wait upon you with an assistant. I have said enough to convince you of my knowledge, and merely inform you that you can, when you answer, be as brief as possible.

Direct yours to
CHARLES GRANT JR., of Prospect, Maine.

Knapp was baffled by the letter; he had never heard of Charles Grant and had no idea what he was implying. He took it to his son, Joseph Jr., who said that it contained "a lot of trash" and suggested he give the letter to the Vigilance Committee.

Soon, two more letters arrived in Salem from Charles Grant Jr. One was addressed to Honorable Gideon Barstow, chairman of the Vigilance Committee:

May 13, 1830.

Gentlemen of the Committee of Vigilance:—Hearing that you have taken up four young men on suspicion of being concerned in the murder of Mr. White, I think it time to inform you that Steven White came to me one night and told me, if I would remove the old gentleman, he would give me five thousand dollars; he said he was afraid he would alter his will if he lived any longer. I told him I would do it, but I was afeared to go into the house, so he said he would go with me, that he would try to get into the house in the evening and open the window, would then go home and go to bed and meet me again about eleven. I found him, and we both went into his chamber. I struck him on the head with a heavy piece of lead, and then stabbed him with a dirk; he made the finishing strokes with another. He promised to send me the money next evening, and has not sent it yet, which is the reason that I mention this.

Yours, etc.,
GRANT.

Stephen White was a nephew of the murdered man and his principal heir. He received a letter from Mr. Grant as well:

Lynn, May 12, 1830.

Mr. White will send the $5000, or a part of it, before to-morrow night, or suffer the painful consequences.

GRANT.

After seeing the first letter to Joseph Knapp Sr., the Vigilance Committee sent a response. It also sent a man to Prospect, Maine, who explained the situation to the postmaster and hid in the post office, waiting for Grant to pick up his mail. Grant was arrested the same day and proved to be an ex-convict whose real name was Palmer and was living in the adjoining town of Belfast, Maine. He had been an associate of George and Richard Crowninshield and was in their house when he heard Frank Knapp ask Richard Crowninshield to kill Captain White, saying his brother Joseph would pay $1,000 for the job. When Palmer heard that White had been murdered, he sent the letter to blackmail Joseph Knapp; however, unaware that there were two Joseph Knapps, he sent the letter to the wrong one.

Palmer was detained as a witness, and warrants were issued for the arrests of John Francis Knapp and Joseph Jenkins Knapp Jr. Fearing he might be

Gardiner-Pingree House, Salem, where Captain White was murdered. *Photo by Peter Meo.*

implicated as well, a young man came forward to say that Joseph Jr. had given him two letters to mail. The letter to the Vigilance Committee and the letter to Stephen White proved to be written in Joseph's hand.

After three days in Jail, Joseph Knapp confessed. He said he knew that Captain White had made out a will bequeathing his mother-in-law, Mrs. Beckford, $15,000. He believed that if White died without a will, she would receive $200,000 and his family would be made for life. Knapp was a frequent visitor to White's house and always had access. Four days before the murder, he was in the house, went to Captain White's chamber, found the key to his iron chest, opened it and found the will, which he carried away and destroyed. Then, with his brother's help, he negotiated with Richard Crowninshield to kill White for $1,000.

They agreed that the murder would be done on the night of April 6. Joseph persuaded his mother-in-law to spend a few days at his home in Wenham. On the day of April 6, he went back into White's house and unfastened the rear parlor window. About ten o'clock that night, Crowninshield met Frank in front of the house, and after all the lights had been extinguished, Frank watched as Crowninshield climbed the plank and entered the parlor window. Later, Crowninshield met Frank in a side street and told him he had struck Captain White with a bludgeon on the left temple, probably killing him instantly. To make sure he was dead, he pulled down the sheets and stabbed him repeatedly in the heart. He then hid the bludgeon under the steps of the meetinghouse on Howard Street.

Joseph admitted that the story he and his brother had told the Vigilance Committee about being robbed on the road to Wenham had been a lie. He also admitted to writing the second two letters and signing Grant's name.

It is not surprising that Richard Crowninshield had been hired as the Knapps' hit man. He was the leader of a gang of thieves, centered in Danvers, who had been terrorizing Essex County for the previous ten years. Crowninshield, who was from wealthy parents of Liverpool, England, was born while the family was visiting Europe. They settled in Massachusetts when Richard was two years old. At age ten, he was enrolled in the pubic grammar school in Danvers, but within a few months, he had been expelled for being unruly and mischievous. He was later sent to a private school in New Hampshire in preparation for attending Harvard University. After a series of pranks, he was expelled from that school as well.

When he returned to Danvers, his father secured him a position under a clerk in a factory, but it was not long before he resumed his previous deviltry. He continued his pranks and practical jokes—such as appearing at a dance held a neighbor's house dressed as a woman—until he became a social outcast, shunned by decent society. Then, at age eighteen, all the humor left his antics and he became a professional criminal.

Dick Crowninshield became the leader of a gang of thieves and highwaymen whose hideout was a cave in Wenham Woods, an area that the God-fearing avoided. The gang flourished for several years, with Crowninshield the undisputed leader until he seduced a neighbor's daughter. When she died in childbirth, he decided it was a good time to leave Wenham, and armed with letters of introduction from some of his prominent friends, Richard Crowninshield fled to Charleston, South Carolina.

There, he fell in love with the seventeen-year-old daughter of a wealthy planter, and she fell in love with him. They planned to marry, and the girl's father was ready to give his blessing until he used his contacts in Massachusetts to check the character of Richard Crowninshield. When he learned the truth, the father forbade the marriage and barred Crowninshield from the house. Allegedly, the couple planned to elope, but she suffered a sudden and untimely death.

Crowninshield returned to Danvers a broken man. In a Salem neighborhood known as South Fields, he opened a gambling house where large sums of money were known to change hands. It was a place where sharpers, harlots and cutthroats from Salem, Lynn and Danvers would assemble. It was here that the Knapp brothers came to hire a killer.

Richard Crowninshield, who had maintained an attitude of indifference throughout his incarceration, collapsed when he learned of Knapp's confession. Though no one in his gang would dare give information against him, Crowninshield had no such hold on the Knapps; he had no defense against their accusations. The authorities recovered a quantity of stolen property in Crowninshield's barn and found the bludgeon under the meetinghouse steps. On June 15, Richard Crowninshield committed suicide by hanging himself to the bars of his cell with a handkerchief.

Crowninshield's death greatly complicated the state's case against the Knapps. They had been indicted as accessories in the murder of Captain Joseph White, but by the letter of the law, they could not be tried as accessories until the principal had been convicted. Crowninshield's suicide guaranteed that this would not happen. Attempting to beat the odds against them, the state engaged the prominent statesman, lawyer and orator Daniel Webster to prosecute John Francis Knapp.

Webster had been a congressman from New Hampshire before moving to Boston in 1816. Over the next six years, he successfully argued a number of cases before the United States Supreme Court, establishing himself as the

Daniel Webster. *Wikimedia Commons.*

nation's leading attorney. In 1823, he was elected to Congress from Boston, and in 1827, he was elected a United States senator from Massachusetts. He was a sitting senator at the time of Knapp's trial.

Though Webster had earned his reputation as a defense attorney, he had little trouble transferring his skills to the prosecution of John Knapp. In his opening, he summed up the unique aspects of the crime:

> *Gentlemen, it is a most extraordinary case. In some respects, it has hardly a precedent anywhere; certainly none in our New England history. This bloody drama exhibited no suddenly excited, ungovernable rage. The actors in it were not surprised by any lion-like temptation springing upon their virtue, and overcoming it, before resistance could begin. Nor did they do the deed to glut savage vengeance, or satiate long-settled and deadly hate. It was a cool, calculating, money-making murder. It was all "hire and salary, not revenge." It was the weighing of money against life; the counting out of so many pieces of silver against so many ounces of blood.*

He equated Crowninshield's suicide with a confession:

The human heart was not made for the residence of such an inhabitant. It finds itself preyed on by a torment, which it dares not acknowledge to God or man. A vulture is devouring it, and it can ask no sympathy or assistance, either from heaven or earth. The secret which the murderer possesses soon comes to possess him, and leads him whithersoever it will. He feels it beating at his heart, rising to his throat, and demanding disclosure. He thinks the whole world sees it in his face, reads it in his eyes, and almost hears its workings in the very silence of his thoughts. It has become his master. It betrays his discretion, it breaks down his courage, it conquers his prudence. When suspicions from without begin to embarrass him, and the net of circumstance to entangle him, the fatal secret struggles with still greater violence to burst forth. It must be confessed, it will be confessed; there is no refuge from confession but suicide, and suicide is confession.

In the end, the jury could not agree on a verdict, and a retrial was held. The second jury found John Francis Knapp guilty of murder and sentenced him to death. Joseph J. Knapp Jr. was tried and found guilty as well. Charges were dropped against George Crowninshield, the killer's brother.

On September 28, 1830, thousands of people witnessed the hanging of John Francis Knapp and Joseph Jenkins Knapp in Salem. The brothers were hanged together from the same gallows.

THE BALLAD OF JOSEPH WHITE

Murder ballads were never as popular in New England as they were in the southern Appalachians, but the murder of Joseph White inspired this anonymous ballad, sung to the tune of "Auld Lang Syne." This song was printed in *American Murder Ballads and Their Stories* by Olive Woolley Burt, who edited out seven verses:

The Ballad of Joseph White

O what a horrid tale to sound
In this our land to tell,
That Joseph White of Salem Town
By ruffian hands he fell!

Perhaps for money or for gain
This wicked deed was done;
But if for either, great the pain
This murderer must be in

Oh the infernal of the damn'd,
To murder in the night;
With cruel arm and bloodstain'd hand
Which pierc'd the side of White.
Thou harden'd hearted monster devil,
To thrust the dirk of death,
You will be plac'd upon the level.
For time will stop your breath!

(three stanzas omitted)

Calmly he laid in sweet repose,
The ruffian forced the room,
And with his dirk he did dispose
Of him who'd done no harm.
Great God, how can these things be so,
When man is left alone?
Poor feeble wretch, he does not know
How wicked he has done.

(Last four stanzas omitted)

CIRCUMSTANTIAL
EVIDENCE
ROCKPORT, 1877, AND LYNNFIELD, 1897

A ny murder case without an eyewitness must be prosecuted by indirect, or circumstantial, evidence. The prosecution attempts to present to the jury an interlocking chain of facts that, when viewed together, implicates the accused and no one else. Before the twentieth century, the tools for providing these facts were very limited. There was no fingerprint identification and no blood typing; in fact, it was impossible to tell for sure if a bloodstain was even human blood. Ballistics and forensic medicine were in their nascent stages and provided only the most general evidence. Often, the outcome of a trial depended on the relative skill of the attorneys involved to present or refute a chain of suppositions.

In most cases, the evidence was clear enough that when a jury of twelve men unanimously declared the defendant guilty or innocent, the community was satisfied that justice was done. When a person was found guilty of first-degree murder and sentenced to hang, he or she was strongly urged, by lawmen and clergy, to confess the crime. More often than not, the condemned prisoner did confess, and the community could take comfort in the knowledge that they were not executing an innocent person.

But what happened when the condemned would not confess? What if there were lingering doubts about the evidence and the convicted man continued to profess innocence? This would be tested in two Essex County convictions in the late 1800s. In 1877, Albert F. Joy was convicted of killing Charles H. Gilman, even though the evidence was extremely indirect, and Joy had no apparent motive—"A murder without a cause," the *Boston Daily Globe* called it. Twenty years later, Alfred C. Williams was convicted of killing John Gallo on evidence so thin that his attorney could make a compelling argument that no crime had been committed at all. In each case, the condemned man staunchly maintained his innocence, but for each, the results would be profoundly different.

THE MURDER OF CHARLES H. GILMAN

On the morning of April 11, 1877, five men got off the nine o'clock train at Rockport Depot. Rockport is a small, picturesque town on the tip of Cape Ann, which, in 1877, was known primarily for fishing. Three of the men who got off the train were fishermen, who proceeded to Pigeon Cove hoping to get work on a fishing boat. The other two were traveling salesmen dealing in sewing machine attachments. Charles H. Gilman, in his mid-twenties, and his twenty-one-year-old assistant, Albert C. Joy, were traveling through Essex County for a manufacturer in Lowell. They had spent the previous day in Beverly and had come to Rockport to sell thread-cutter attachments.

Gilman and Joy went their separate ways that morning in Rockport. Charles Gilman was calling at Rockport homes, working from a list of prospective buyers. At about 10:30 a.m., he stopped at the house of Mrs. Catherine E. Holmes and sold her a thread-cutter. Mrs. Holmes paid with a ten-dollar bill and noticed that the salesman added her bill to a roll of bills

Pigeon Cove, Rockport. *Library of Congress.*

he was carrying. Albert Joy was not selling that morning; he spent the time shopping for a gun. Joy visited at least six stores in Rockport, looking for a pistol in the three- to four-dollar range, but had no luck.

At 10:40 a.m., Joy was back at the depot, where he spoke with a man named James Robinson. Joy told Robinson he was a salesman for a sewing machine company and he was waiting for Charles Gilman—who he sometimes referred to as his boss, sometimes as his chum. He was planning to have dinner with Gilman before taking the next train back to Gloucester. When Joy saw Gilman through the window, he got up and left the depot.

According to Joy, he asked Gilman if he wanted to get dinner, and Gilman said he only wanted a drink of water. Joy said they should go to the reservoir, up a hill not far from the depot, as the water in the depot was not very good. The two men went to the reservoir, and Gilman drank and then said to Joy, "Go and get dinner, and I will go to these houses," indicating a few more sales calls he wished to make.

Joy went alone, down the hill, in a different direction than the way he had come. He stopped at a restaurant near the depot and ordered oyster stew and asked if they had a brush and some shoe blacking for his boots. The waiter brought them but noticed that Joy's boots were too wet to polish; he also noticed that his sleeve was wet. Joy left the restaurant without eating the stew.

Sometime between noon and 1:00 p.m., eighteen-year-old George R. Doyle, returning from a "gunning expedition" that morning, stopped at the reservoir for a drink. He saw some clothing floating near the shore and on closer inspection realized it was actually a dead body. Doyle hurried into town and told Constable Eben Blatchford. He led Blatchford back to the scene, and before long, a small crowd had gathered around the dead man.

While this was going on, Albert Joy sat in the smoking car of the train preparing to leave Rockport Depot for Gloucester. James Robinson, the man Joy had been talking to earlier in the day, entered the car and, surprised to see Joy sitting there, said, "I thought you was dead."

Joy asked why he would think him dead, and Robinson replied that he had been told that a sewing machine man had been found dead in the reservoir, and he thought it must be Joy.

"My God, it's my chum!" Joy exclaimed and then hurried off the train and up to the reservoir.

The body had been removed from the water, and Joy rushed up and wiped his face with a handkerchief, saying, "My God, Charlie, is that you?"

Charles Gilman's body was taken first to the Odd Fellows Hall after it was learned that Gilman had been a member of that order and then to city hall for examination. Dr. J.E. Sanborn examined the body, assisted by three other Rockport medical men; all concurred that Gilman had died from drowning after being hit on the head by a rock or club. He was either unconscious when he hit the water or his head was held under water until he drowned.

Albert Joy was taken to the police station for questioning, and there he began telling false and conflicting stories. First, he claimed that his name was William Williams. He was in police custody for a full day before they learned his real name. At the restaurant, he had claimed that he had come from Lewiston, Maine, to join a fishing vessel called the *Eldora* but found that it was in Newburyport, not Rockport. The police found that his pant legs and sleeves were wet. Joy first said he did not know how his sleeves came to be wet and then later said he had been rowing in a dory in Gloucester the previous day and had to bail water. There were bloodstains on Joy's coat that he explained had come from a horse when he had recently worked at a stable.

Joy told the police that the three fishermen who had gotten off the train with them had asked Gilman about his work and whether it paid well. He claimed the three men had dogged Gilman as he made his sales calls. Joy was sure that they were the killers. As strangers in town, the three fishermen were held as witnesses but later released. Joy was arrested and taken to Salem jail.

The question of Charles Gilman's money has prompted the *Boston Daily Globe* to say that if Joy was guilty, it was "a murder without any cause." Joy and other witnesses claimed that Gilman had been carrying a large sum of money. Gilman had only seventeen dollars in his pocket when he was found. His pocketbook and hat had been hidden in the rocks not far from the body, and the pocketbook was empty. But when Albert Joy was searched, he was only carrying sixteen dollars. The roll of bills Gilman had been seen carrying earlier in the day was missing. Nevertheless, Joy was charged with murder, and robbery was given as the motive.

Albert Joy appeared haggard when his case came to trial that July. He was to be tried by the supreme judicial court in Salem, Judges Morton and Lord presiding. Three months in the Salem jail had taken a toll on his body and mind. The *Boston Daily Globe* said, "His eyes look sunken and his aspect is forbidding, much more so than when first arrested." Joy would be prosecuted by Attorney General Charles J. Train and District Attorney Edgar J. Sherman. He was represented by three prominent attorneys: W.D. Northend of Salem and Charles Thompson and Henri Wood of Gloucester.

The first day of the trial, the jury heard the state's opening address, delivered by Mr. Sherman, and then they were taken by train to Rockport to see the site of the murder. The prosecution contended that while Gilman was making his sales calls, Joy was trying to procure a weapon and trying to find a suitable location for the murder. The two men were seen going up the hill to the reservoir together, but only one came down. Joy had killed his boss, taken his money and, under questioning, had told conflicting stories, trying to pin the blame on innocent people. The prosecution called at least fifty witnesses in the four days of the trial.

The defense contended that Joy had left the reservoir before the murder was committed. They presented a witness who, at 12:45 p.m.—after Joy had left the hill—saw what she "took to be a boy jumping from a rock on the hill; he was in his shirt sleeves." Other than that, they offered no new evidence. In his closing argument for the defense, Mr. Northend said it was "ridiculously improbable" that Joy, if intent on murder, would advertise his intention by trying to buy a pistol at six different places. The same was true for selecting the reservoir as a murder site; prior to taking Gilman there, Joy had told several people that he intended to go there for water.

The case was given to the jury at 12:20 p.m. on July 12, 1877, and at 2:30 p.m., they returned with a verdict of guilty. There had been no dissension in the jury room; they took an informal vote when they entered, and all twelve voted guilty. They then reviewed the evidence to see if any doubt would emerge. After two more unanimous votes, the jury was ready to find Albert Joy guilty of first-degree murder. Judge Morton asked Joy if he had anything to say, and Joy declined. The judge then pronounced the sentence, saying that the verdict had been in accordance with the evidence and facts. Joy was to be taken back to jail and held until October 19 and then to be hanged by the neck until dead.

But not everyone was as convinced as the judge and jury that the verdict was "in accordance with the evidence and facts." As the execution date approached, a petition drive led by Albert Joy's mother and supported by prominent Essex County men such as G.J.L. Colby, editor of the *Newburyport Herald*, succeeded in getting a hearing before the governor and the executive council to ask for a pardon. They did not win a pardon, but the execution was reprieved until December 14. The drive continued, and on December 6, 1877, the executive council commuted the death sentence of Albert Joy to life imprisonment.

In 1877, life imprisonment meant just that—behind bars for the rest of your natural life—but Mrs. Joy continued to work for the release of her boy. She finally succeeded in July 1895, when Albert Joy was pardoned and released from prison. The pardon was agreed to because of the lingering doubt surrounding the case and because of Albert Joy's good behavior during his sixteen years of incarceration.

THE MURDER OF JOHN GALLO

When Alfred C. Williams was arrested for the murder of John Gallo, his conviction seemed highly unlikely. There appeared to be no direct link between Williams and Gallo. There was no absolute proof that Gallo had been murdered or even that he was dead. But in this case, circumstantial evidence actually succeeded in dispelling doubt, bringing investigators closer to the truth and drawing the noose ever tighter around Alfred Williams's neck.

John Gallo was a young Italian immigrant who worked on the farm of Warren W. Phillips in Lynnfield, taking care of livestock and doing general farm labor. He was industrious and popular with the other workers but kept to himself and very seldom left the farm. Gallo lived alone in a small shack in the rear of the farm. In the early hours of July 28, 1897, the shack caught fire and burned with flames so high they could be seen in neighboring towns. The shack was leveled, leaving nothing but ashes and the charred remains of a body, so badly burned that it could not be identified.

As was common at the time, Mr. Phillips did not live on the farm he owned; he lived in the town of Swampscott, leaving the management of the farm to Fred Gray, the foreman. Gray and his family lived in a large farmhouse near the road between Lynnfield Center and Wakefield. Behind the house were a barn for the cattle and a stable for the horses and carriages. Behind the stable was the two-room cottage where Gallo lived, consisting of a main room, about ten feet square, connected to a lean-to about eight feet by ten feet. He did his own cooking on a stove in the larger room and slept in the lean-to.

The fire was so devastating that every piece of wood in the building was reduced to ashes. The body was so charred that it took two examinations to verify that it was, in fact, the body of a human. The head and neck were gone and both arms and both legs had been completely consumed, bone and all, by the fire. The spinal column remained with some back muscle attached; the heart, liver, kidneys and bladders remained but were badly burned. Everything else was completely gone. The medical examiner could furnish no information beyond the fact that the body was that of an adult human being.

With the destruction of the shack so complete, it, at first, appeared to investigators that nothing could be learned to explain what had happened that night. But as the investigation progressed, details began to emerge, like an image developing on a photographic plate. The fact that there was too little information became a clue in itself, and soon investigators were able to compile a list of facts that pointed to foul play:

1. The body had been destroyed to a greater extent than would be expected from a fire in such a small building. It would have taken intense heat to consume the limbs—bones and all.
2. The occupant of the house had not been burned in bed. The bedsprings had survived the blaze, but the body was found several feet away.
3. The victim had not been wearing clothes at the time of death. Some buckles, metal buttons, a few coins and the clasp of a pocketbook were found by the side of the bedsprings; none was found near the body.
4. The body lay in the doorway between rooms with the head back in the room toward the bed, not falling forward as a person would naturally fall if trying to escape from a burning room. Several people who had witnessed the fire said that it had begun in the sleeping room.
5. A kerosene oil can, which was usually kept near the stove, was found in the middle of the floor next to the body.

It was now believed that the victim had been murdered before the fire started. His body was doused with kerosene and ignited, which would account for the severe damage to the body. The flame then quickly spread to the rest of the house.

John Gallo had earned $1.50 a day at Phillips's farm and was paid monthly, always in $5 bills. He spent very little, and at the time of his death, it was suspected that he had in the shack about $100 earned on the farm. If the paper money had been in the shack, it would have burned in the fire, but it was also well known that Gallo always carried three $20 gold pieces that he had earned on a construction job prior to coming to the farm. The ashes were thoroughly searched, and no trace of the gold pieces or any melted gold was found. It was believed that Gallo had been murdered for his money.

Another crime had allegedly been committed near Lynnfield in the early morning of July 28, around the time of the fire. Later that afternoon, Alfred C. Williams reported that he had been held up near his rooming house in Wakefield. He had been unable to sleep and went outside to smoke a cigar. He lit the cigar and walked down the road near Wakefield Pond. As he stood with one foot on the rail fence by the road, someone suddenly struck him on the head from behind. He turned to fight back, striking his assailant on the nose and causing it to bleed. A fight ensued, and Williams was getting the best of his opponent when a second assailant struck him from behind. He was knocked unconscious, robbed of his watch and a small amount of money and then thrown down the banks of Wakefield Pond. He awoke

SCENE OF THE ALLEGED ASSAULT ON WILLIAMS.

Boston Daily Globe, *July 30, 1897.*

about four o'clock in the morning and found himself lying with one arm in the pond. He made his way alone to his boardinghouse with no idea that just a mile away in Lynnfield, John Gallo's shack was burning down.

He told his story to the Wakefield chief of police and State Officer Neal. Williams showed them bruises on his neck and face from the fight and bloodstains on his clothing from the assailant's nose. The officers were skeptical of his story and held Williams for questioning. Unlike most holdups, Williams apparently had more money in his possession after the crime than he had before. On July 27, it was known that Williams had not had enough money to buy a meal or even pay a five-cent streetcar fare. The morning of July 28, he paid his back board bill and made some purchases, and the police found seventy-five dollars, in five-dollar bills, on his person. Williams first claimed the money had been sent to him in a registered letter from his brother to help finance a planned trip to the Klondike gold fields. But after realizing how easy it would be to check this with the post office, he changed his story and claimed he had found the money.

Circumstantial Evidence

Alfred Williams was an immigrant as well; he and his brother John had come to Massachusetts from Prince Edward Island. Alfred was strong and clean-cut. It was remarked at the time that he had "a face free from the ugly, dark, vindictive, quarrelsome look often seen on the faces of criminals." He had no history of trouble with the law.

The police learned that Williams had previously worked as a laborer on Phillips's farm and knew the habits of the deceased. All the workers on the farm knew that Gallo carried three gold pieces, and everyone seemed to know that he kept a large amount of paper currency in his shack. In one of the buildings on the farm, the police found a pair of bloodstained pants belonging to Williams. They searched his room, and in a corner, under the carpet, they found two twenty-dollar gold pieces. When Williams was told where they found the coins, he responded, "I know, I put them there." They also found a bloodstained coat and vest in his room. Williams claimed the stains were from the attacker whose nose he had bloodied, but the police did not buy it. Alfred C. Williams was arrested for the murder of John Gallo.

Williams was given the option to plead guilty to second-degree murder, but he declined. His trial for first-degree murder, held in Salem, began on February 7, 1898. The court was prepared for a long trial, and for the first time, the jury would be housed in the Essex House hotel for the duration of the trial rather than sleeping in the courtroom, as juries had in previous cases. A large crowd was waiting on Federal Street to view the trial, but the number of spectators would be limited to the number of seats in the courtroom—no one would be allowed to stand. During the proceedings, Williams was seated inside a cage on the right side of the courtroom, above the bar.

The prosecution presented a case against Williams that was based entirely on circumstantial evidence. While there was nothing to directly link Williams to the fire, his familiarity with Gallo's habits, his possession of money—including gold pieces—the day after the fire, the bloody clothing and Williams's inconsistent stories, taken all together, were incriminating.

With what the *Boston Globe* called a "masterly argument," Williams's attorney challenged the very core of the evidence. There was no proof that the body found in the ashes was John Gallo's; it was so badly charred that the medical examiner could not even be sure of the sex of the victim. It could not be proven that a murder was committed or that the fire was not started accidentally. There was no proof that Alfred Williams was anywhere near the fire that night. But Williams was sticking to the story that he was held up on the night of July 28, so his alibi was also a matter of circumstantial evidence. He could not prove that he was held up and left unconscious that night, and no one seemed willing to believe it.

The jury deliberated for six hours. At one point, they asked the judge for a clarification on a point of law: "If a man went to a house to rob or plunder and a murder was committed, would that be murder in the first degree?" The judge responded that a murder committed during the course of a robbery would, indeed, be first-degree murder. The jury deliberated a few minutes more and then, at 10:55 p.m. on February 10, 1898, they returned with a verdict of guilty of first-degree murder.

In May 1898, the case was appealed to the supreme judicial court on the grounds that there was no direct evidence that a crime had been committed; that there was no link between the gold pieces found in Williams's room and the gold pieces allegedly carried by the deceased; and that the evidence of what Williams said to the officers searching his room was not admissible. The court ruled that the habits of the missing man, taken together with the appearance and conduct of the defendant, were sufficient to prove that the man was murdered and murdered by the defendant. The gold pieces, as well, were admissible because of the known habits of the deceased and the conduct of the defendant. And, on an indictment for murder, evidence of what the defendant said to the officer is admissible.

Williams tried again to ask for a new trial but was refused. Since Governor Walcott showed no inclination toward pardoning him, Williams's fate was sealed. Alfred C. Williams was hanged in the yard of Salem jail on October 7, 1898. It was not a public hanging; the sheriff issued a few invitations but only for the purpose of providing legal witnesses. Williams's arms and legs were bound, and his head was covered as he stood on the gallows. At 10:01 a.m., the trap was sprung, and Williams dropped six feet, one inch. His neck was broken, and he died within seconds. Williams professed innocence to the end, but the evidence against him was more convincing.

DRIVEN BY DELUSION

LAWRENCE, 1885

O n August 29, 1885, Henry Goodwin went into the office of the L. Sprague Manufacturing Company—a maker of bobbins, spools and shuttles for the textile industry—on Lowell Street in Lawrence, Massachusetts. Goodwin was not an employee of L. Sprague, but he was well known in the office and had prior business dealings with Albert Swan, treasurer of the company and the man he had come to see. Swan's office was separated by a panel of glass from the office of Elbridge Osgood, the clerk of the concern. Goodwin said good morning to Osgood, and they briefly passed the time before Goodwin went into Swan's office and closed the door.

About half an hour later, Eldridge Osgood heard a gunshot on the other side of the glass partition. He looked up and, through the glass, saw smoke by Albert Swan's head. Swan was leaning on his desk, trying to stand, and then he fell backward onto the floor. Osgood ran to the door and shouted, "Al, what is the matter?"

Goodwin passed him as Osgood went through the office door. Osgood said, "Henry, what is the matter?"

Henry Goodwin responded, "I have shot him, I meant to do it."

Osgood ran out of the office to get the doctor. Hearing the commotion, Enoch Coburn, the president of L. Sprague, came into Osgood's office, along with several men from the mill. They heard Goodwin talking on the telephone in the corner of Osgood's office; he was calling the police. He told the police that he had shot Albert Swan and wanted to know if he should wait for them or go to the police station himself. Coburn ran into Swan's

The murder of
Albert Swan.
By Tom Wilhelm.

office and saw blood spattered on the wall and Swan lying on the ground, still breathing, his head in a puddle of blood eighteen inches wide and an inch deep. Osgood returned and held onto Swan's wrist, feeling his pulse until it beat no more.

Apparently, the police told Goodwin to come in himself, because that is what he did. On Lowell Street, he met a man in a carriage and asked for a ride to the police station. They stopped first at a stable run by Goodwin's uncle, Joseph Stowell. There he left the revolver he had used in the murder and a long dirk he had been carrying as well. Goodwin walked to the police station, and when he entered, he announced, "I have come to give myself up. I have shot Al Swan."

A policeman asked him why, and Goodwin responded, "I told him a year ago that unless he came to some settlement with me about our matters, I would have his heart's blood. He has robbed me of my papers and my patents, and when I have undertaken to sell them I could not give a good title. He has robbed me of $40,000. I did it, I meant to do it, and I am here to take the consequences."

"Is he dead?" someone asked.

"I don't know," Goodwin responded, "but no man who was shot in the back of the head, as I shot Al Swan, was ever known to live. I went down there this morning to kill him and I did it. I am now ready to take the consequences."

The papers and patents in question had to do with telephone equipment. Henry Goodwin was an electrical engineer who had developed several enhancements to the newly invented device, including a revolutionary switchboard that would automatically route up to six hundred telephone calls.

The city of Lawrence was an early adopter of the new communication technology. It is not surprising, since the city had grown up along with the telegraph. Lawrence was founded in 1845—the same year that the first commercial telegraph line was installed. A group of entrepreneurs purchased land in Methuen and Andover, along the Merrimack River, planning to take advantage of the energy potential in the five-thousand-foot drop in elevation of the Merrimack River from its source to the sea. What was vacant land in 1845 had, in thirty years, grown into one of the largest industrial centers in America with a population of over thirty-eight thousand people. In 1876, Alexander Graham Bell gave the first public demonstration of the telephone. In 1878, the first telephone system in Lawrence—the Lawrence Telephone Exchange—was established by Henry K. Goodwin and his business partner, a Mr. Caldwell.

Henry Goodwin had grown up in Lawrence, brought to town when he was two years old by his widowed mother. She had come from Vermont to live with her brother Joseph Stowell. Goodwin went to public school in Lawrence, where he met and became friends with Albert Swan. Henry Goodwin was fifteen years old when the Civil War broke out; he enlisted and fought with the Army of the Potomac. In 1863, he was taken prisoner of war and spent time in several Confederate prisons, including five months in Andersonville, a prison notorious for starving and abusing inmates. Sometime later, he was included in a prisoner exchange, selected primarily because he appeared to be on the verge of death. A shadow of his former self, sickly, emaciated and unable to walk without help, Henry Goodwin was brought home to Lawrence to die.

But under the care of his family, Goodwin's health improved enough for him to return to military service until he was honorably mustered out in 1865. After the war, Goodwin learned the trade of harness making from his uncle. When he had learned all that his uncle had to teach him, Goodwin went to Boston and found a teacher who would help him perfect his harness-making skills. This would be a recurring characteristic of Goodwin's personality: when he undertook any activity, he did it with single-minded dedication,

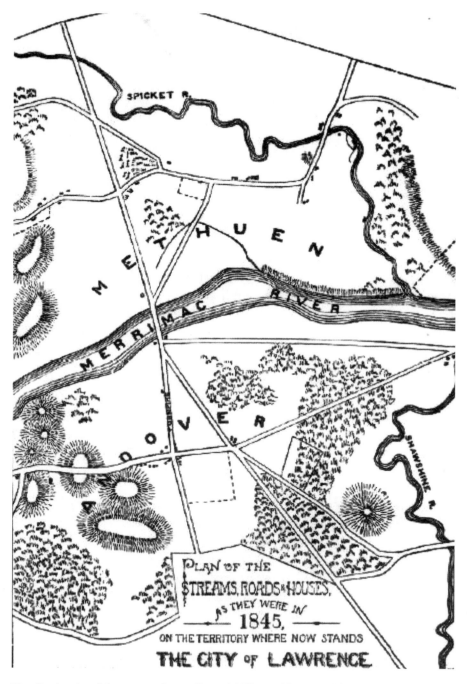

Plan for the city of Lawrence. *Quarter-Centennial History of Lawrence, Massachusetts.*

working with all his heart, not content with mere superficial knowledge but striving to become as proficient as possible.

Another notable aspect of Henry Goodwin's personality was the fact that once he reached a level of expertise that satisfied him, he would completely abandon the subject and focus his energy on something else. Once he had mastered harness making, Goodwin turned his attention to music, mastering not just one instrument but all instruments that he could acquire, sometimes ordering instruments from as far away as Germany. Then, just as suddenly as he had abandoned harness making, he abandoned music for the study of telegraphy. He learned not just the art of sending and receiving coded messages but also the mechanics and engineering of the devices themselves. From here, it was a small step to the new science of telephony.

In 1878, with investment capital from his uncle, Goodwin and Caldwell started the Lawrence Telephone Exchange, a telephone system where subscribers communicated with one another through a central office. To facilitate this, Goodwin invented switches and a switchboard allowing automatic connections. In 1880, they sold the Lawrence Telephone Exchange to the Bell Telephone Company, which immediately resold it to Albert Swan and his partner, William Knox. Goodwin continued to work evenings for the exchange, but during the day, he went to the Institute of Technology in Boston to further his education in the theory of electricity.

He stayed at the institute for about a year and then contracted to travel to South America to develop telephone systems in Uruguay and Argentina. In 1881, he traveled to Buenos Aires with his cousin Frank E. Stowell. It was there that another, darker characteristic of Henry Goodwin's personality emerged—an incessant fear that those around him were conspiring to steal his work. After several months in Argentina, he began to suspect that the men he was working for were trying to learn the secrets of his switching system. The fear became so intense that he tore up a very lucrative contract and refused to do any more work for the company.

Goodwin went to work for a rival company in Buenos Aires, run by a man named Fells. The first company, with an unfinished system that it was unable to complete, offered him $4,000 to return. When Goodwin refused, the company offered him $4,240, part of it in gold, if he would return for just six evenings of work. He refused this as well. Finally, it offered him $4,000 if he would quit the rival company and leave the country forever. He did not accept this offer either.

Throughout these exchanges, Frank Stowell was pressing his cousin to accept the offers. But Goodwin took his insistence as betrayal and accused

ALBERT DAVID SWAN,

Quarter-Centennial History of Lawrence, Massachusetts.

Stowell of conspiring with the first company to steal his ideas. Seeing the situation as hopeless, Stowell left South America, leaving Goodwin by himself. Then, as suddenly as he left the first company, Goodwin left the employ of Mr. Fells, claiming he was owed $5,000 that Fells would not pay. Goodwin went to work for a man named Powers. Then, in September 1883, for no apparent reason, he quit Powers and returned to Lawrence.

Back in Lawrence, Goodwin found that his old friend Albert Swan was now associated with the Molecular Telephone Company, a New York manufacturing concern with some innovative telephone products. While Swan was a businessman with vision, he knew nothing of electricity and was happy to have Goodwin back to advise him. Swan was able to get his friend a position with the Molecular Telephone Company.

Swan also helped Goodwin patent some of his inventions. They agreed to share the patents, fifty-fifty, and Swan went forward with the paperwork. They submitted three patents; one was rejected because it had already been patented by someone else, but the other two were accepted. A patent was granted for a new switch Goodwin had invented, but for his most important invention, his switchboard, a patent was not obtained because Swan had failed to pay the final fee on time. In the meantime, Henry Waite, a practical electrician working for Molecular Telephone, successfully patented a similar switchboard. For once, Goodwin may have been correct in suspecting that others, including his friend Al Swan, had conspired to steal his ideas. The matter was resolved by establishing a company where Goodwin, Swan, Waite and an officer of Molecular Telephone named Charles Livermore would each own one-quarter of the patent. Swan was to pay Goodwin for development expenses, and Livermore was to pay Waite.

This agreement seemed to placate Goodwin for a time. He remained employed by the Molecular Telephone Company, but he repeatedly called on

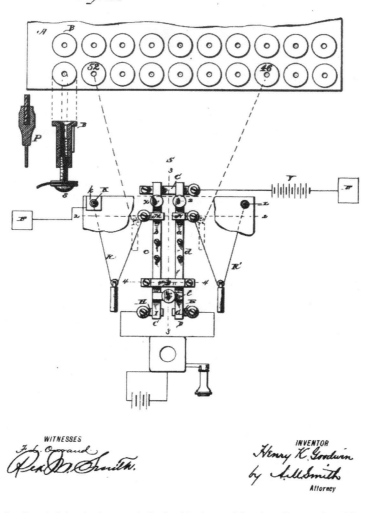

(No Model.)

H. K. GOODWIN.

TELEPHONE SWITCH.

2 Sheets—Sheet 1.

No. 302,330.

Patented July 22, 1884.

WITNESSES

INVENTOR

Henry K. Goodwin

by A. McSmith
Attorney

Patent for Goodwin's telephone switch. *Specifications and drawings of patents issued from the United States Patent Office.*

Albert Swan, requesting the shares of stock and expense money he was owed. Swan then secured Goodwin a position as a practical electrician to establish a telephone exchange in Cleveland, Ohio. In Cleveland, the familiar pattern reemerged—Goodwin believed the men there were conspiring to steal his ideas. His delusions had gotten worse; he now believed the Cleveland men were in collusion with Swan and others from Molecular Telephone. He could not look at two men talking without thinking they were talking about him. Goodwin quit Cleveland and returned to Lawrence.

Henry Goodwin continued to demand stock and expenses from Swan but got no satisfaction. In the summer of 1885, he left Lawrence again to look for work on his own. He tried first in Canada and then in Chicago, and in every case—he would later say—someone had written in advance to the place he applied, prejudicing them against him. Finally, he sold his watch, his masonic jewel and other articles of personal property and traveled to Dakota to enlist in the army. He found the conditions at the forts there deplorable, so, in utter despair, he returned again to Lawrence.

He arrived in Lawrence on August 19, ten days before the murder. Goodwin was now in a state of abject poverty and extreme depression. He talked incessantly about how he had been wronged by Albert Swan. When he wasn't talking about his telephone patents, Goodwin talked of plans for murder or suicide. On August 29, he went to the office of Albert Swan and made good on one of the plans.

The trial of Henry K. Goodwin for the murder of Albert D. Swan was held in Salem beginning on December 28, 1885. Edgar J. Sherman, the Essex district attorney who had prosecuted Albert Joy, was now Massachusetts attorney general. Goodwin would be prosecuted by Sherman along with the current district attorney, Henry F. Hurlburt. In addition, the relatives of Albert Swan had hired private council to assist them.

Henry Goodwin was represented, pro bono, by General Benjamin Franklin Butler. Butler had been in the House of Representatives and was governor of Massachusetts between 1883 and 1884. As governor, he made several controversial appointments: the first Irish American and first African American judges in Massachusetts and Clara Barton appointed head of the Massachusetts Reformatory for Women—the first woman appointed to executive office. Butler was also considered a brilliant attorney, but he was most proud of his achievements during the Civil War, most notably leading the force that captured New Orleans. After the war, he would continue to use his military title of general.

Attorney General Sherman had served as a captain under General Butler in New Orleans. After the war, the two remained friends and sometime political allies (Butler had a habit of changing parties). On the occasion of Edgar Sherman's twenty-fifth wedding anniversary, General Butler sent Mrs. Sherman a silver cup and saucer that he had used during the war. But for the duration of this trial, the friendship was strained, and the attacks were sometimes personal.

Before the trial even started, General Butler challenged the jury selection, saying the defendant was denied the right to a jury of his peers, since none of the jurors was from Lawrence or any of the surrounding towns. He also challenged the prosecution's right to investigate the backgrounds of the individual jurors. The judge disagreed on both counts; it was sufficient that the jurors were chosen at random from citizens of Essex County, regardless of their town, and he had no problem with the prosecution investigating the jurors. The defense had the right to do the same.

The fact that Henry Goodwin had murdered Albert Swan was never in question. Though no one had seen him pull the trigger, there were witnesses close enough to know that no one else could have done it. And, of course, Goodwin never denied it; instead, he proclaimed to the world that he had done it and had meant to do it. The prosecution had little to do but relate the facts and present witnesses who had seen what happened that day at the L. Sprague office and who had heard what Henry Goodwin had said.

The defense would claim that Goodwin was not mentally sound when he killed Swan and thus was not guilty of premeditated murder. General Butler presented witnesses who told his story and described his behavior and perceived mental state at the various crisis points in his life. He asserted that Goodwin was predisposed to insanity, bringing witnesses from Vermont to testify to his late father's violent eccentricities and to the uncontrollable insanity of his grandfather and his great-uncle. Goodwin's behavior since his arrest—showing no remorse or apprehension as to his own fate, believing no one could conceive that his act was not perfectly justified—was further proof of mental instability. The defense would assert that Albert Swan had no ill intentions toward his old friend and Goodwin's complaints were all his own delusion.

In his closing argument, General Butler spoke for five hours. He retold Goodwin's story and his family history of insanity. He reiterated all the testimony, accentuating all that would tend to support the claim that Goodwin was insane, acting on delusion rather than fact. He summed up his argument when he said:

> *Why, it was all a delusion, all wrong reasoning; and on that wrong reasoning he put his own life at the same time that he took the life of this man. Judge ye, is my client in the condition of mind that makes deliberately premeditated malice aforethought possible? The deliberation was too great, if that is not a paradox. He pondered it till it grew up to a duty in his mind*

and he was compelled to do it. The delusion had overcome his moral sense; his reasoning powers had long since been overthrown and gone.

Attorney General Sherman's argument took considerably less time than Butler's. He countered the defense by saying that in the three weeks between Goodwin's arrest and the day he engaged an attorney, there had been no mention of insanity or delusion. Everyone in Lawrence knew of the animosity between Goodwin and Swan, and everyone, including friends and relatives, believed the murder had been Goodwin's revenge for the wrongs Swan had done him. "It was as well known in Lawrence then," said Sherman, "that the prisoner and Swan were enemies, as it is that General Butler and I are friends."

He then chastised his friend for relying on prejudice and sympathy by attacking the prosecution before the case had even started, by making sure the jury saw the poor wife of the defendant in court every day, by mentioning Andersonville when he knew one member of the jury had also been imprisoned in Andersonville and by stressing the fact that the defendant had been forced to sell his Masonic jewel when other members of the jury were known Masons. He further challenged the notion that delusion was sufficient to absolve a man from the responsibility of murder. In the prisoner's own words, he had warned Swan a year before that he would be murdered. When the act was committed, he knew there would be consequences and he was ready to accept them.

Sherman had this to say about the charge that Goodwin had inherited insanity from his father:

> *They next say Goodwin's father, Harvey, was peculiar? Wonderful, is it not? It is said in this world that no two men are exactly alike. We are all more or less peculiar. There is no community which does not have men with peculiarities. The world is full of them. If General Butler will excuse me, and I know he will, I will say we have had before us for eight days the most distinguished illustration of a peculiar man. There never was and never will be but one General Butler. He is a great man, possessed of great abilities, with great brain power, and yet his most admiring friend do not claim him to be a man of perfect balance; they believe if he had been that he would have been president long ago.*

The jury retired at six o'clock on the evening of January 5, 1886, and returned between twelve and one o'clock the next afternoon with a verdict

Henry Goodwin at his release from
prison. Lowell Sun, *May 18, 1905.*

of guilty of murder in the second degree. Henry K. Goodwin was sentenced to be confined at the state prison in Charlestown for the duration of his natural life, with the first day in solitary confinement and the remaining days at hard labor.

The trial of Henry Goodwin was General Benjamin Butler's last criminal case. He died in 1893 at age seventy-four. Two years after this case, Edgar Sherman became a justice of the Massachusetts Superior Court, where he spent the rest of his professional career. He spent twenty-four years on the bench and died in 1914 at the age of eighty.

In 1905, after nineteen exemplary years in prison, Henry K. Goodwin was pardoned by the governor. During his stay in Charlestown State Prison, Goodwin had been the chief electrician of the prison and operator of the inter-prison telephone system.

THE BEAUTIFUL
CARRIE ANDREWS
ESSEX, 1894

Thomas Oliver Hazard Perry Burnham was a successful bookseller and publisher in Boston who was born and raised in Essex, a small but prosperous town on the coast of Cape Ann. The Burnhams were an old and prominent family going back to the days when Essex was the Chebacco Parish in Ipswich. Incorporated in 1819, Essex became famous in the nineteenth century for shipbuilding. By the end of the century, over five thousand sailing ships, known for their speed and craftsmanship, were built in the shipyards of Essex. T.O.H.P. Burnham never forgot his roots, and on his death in 1893, he bequeathed $20,000—the worth of a new Essex schooner—to the Town of Essex to build a new town hall and library.

The town embraced the project with enthusiasm. A site was chosen, and the architect Frank Weston was selected in a blind competition. The stones for the foundation were contributed by townspeople, and the clock tower was donated by Lamont Burnham. The *Santa Maria* weather vane at the top commemorates Essex shipbuilding. A dedication ceremony was held on its completion in February 1894.

Scheduled to sing at the ceremony was a bright and vivacious soprano, a rising star from Essex named Carrie Lowe Andrews. Carrie was a beautiful young woman of twenty-five, with dark hair, blue eyes and a perfect complexion. Her voice was beautiful as well, and her singing was in demand at social organizations around the county. Carrie sang for organizations such as Rockport's Rechabite Temple of Honor, a temperance group, and the Murray Club of Gloucester, a literary organization. She was to sing a new

The Beautiful Carrie Andrews

The murder of
Carrie Andrews. *By
Tom Wilhelm*.

piece of music at the library dedication on February 15, a song written for her by Arthur S. Kendall, called "The Fisherman," with lyrics from a poem by Essex County poet John Greenleaf Whittier.

Carrie had recently been going through some turmoil in her personal life. Up until the previous December, she had been in a romantic relationship with Walter Jansen, a salesman of pianos and sewing machines, who lived in Gloucester. Jansen was thirty-five years old and, as a child, had come to America from Germany. In 1894, he had been living in Gloucester for three years. He was tall with a dark complexion, dark hair and a sandy mustache, well dressed with an athletic build. They had met each other at the music store where he worked, and Walter fell madly in love with Carrie. She returned his love, and they soon became engaged. Friends said they were anxious to get married as soon as possible.

Carrie Andrews was from a prominent, successful Essex family. Her father, Timothy Andrews, was the proprietor of the Essex House, the finest hotel in town. She had two uncles who were distinguished businessmen in Gloucester and Somerville. Although Walter Jansen had given Carrie several expensive presents, including a piano, Timothy Andrews was not enthusiastic about his daughter's fiancé. Walter Jansen was insanely jealous and objected to Carrie

T.O.H.P. Burnham Library, Essex. *Photo by Peter Meo.*

being seen in public with any man but himself. More than once he had stormed out of the Andrews's house because other gentlemen were present. Her parents did not approve of Jansen and his erratic behavior, but they felt it best not to interfere. They believed that Carrie would eventually break off the engagement on her own.

Carrie took singing lessons from Mrs. Caroline Munger in Boston, and on several occasions, Walter had followed her by train into Boston to make sure she was remaining faithful. One day, shortly after Christmas 1893, he followed her to Boston and confronted her in the middle of her singing lesson. He called her out and demanded that they be married at once, before returning to Essex. His brother lived on Dwight Street in Boston, and the ceremony could be performed there. Carrie refused, saying she could not consent to be married before June, when her musical education would be complete. Then and there, Walter broke off the engagement and demanded that Carrie send back all the presents he had given her.

This is what Carrie's family had expected from the beginning, and they were relieved that the engagement was finally through. Carrie returned all the gifts and letters Walter Jansen had given her, and her father sent Jansen a letter telling him to send someone to pick up the piano but not to come himself. In another letter, Mr. Andrews wrote "Dear sir—You broke your engagement to my daughter in a most unusual manner and almost tore the ring from Carrie's finger. You must take the consequences, do not bother Carrie further." Mrs. Andrews had a family friend, John Callahan of Haverhill, hand deliver an envelope to Walter Jansen. Inside were Carrie's engagement ring and a note that just said "Finis."

But Jansen had a change of heart and asked Carrie to come back to him. She wrote him a letter saying that he did not seem to realize what he had done and imploring him to give her up. But Walter would not give her up; he was determined to win Carrie back at any cost. He continued to hound Carrie, "making himself very obnoxious to the girl." But the harder he pressed, the more resolute Carrie and her parents became; they were just as determined to remove Walter Jansen from their lives forever.

On February 2, Jansen consulted with his lawyer, A.M. Donahue, and hired him to enter proceedings against Carrie Andrews in court in Gloucester for breach of promise. During his discussions with his attorney, Jansen stated that he intended to shoot his former fiancée. At first, Donahue gave little weight to Jansen's raging, but as he persisted in his threats, Donahue thought it would be prudent to warn someone. He told Carrie's uncle, Charles H. Andrews, about Jansen's threats, and Andrews took the information to the Gloucester city marshal, asking that he lock up Jansen. The marshal refused to do so until there was more evidence that the threats were truly malicious and not just casual remarks of a client to his lawyer.

The following day, Carrie went into Boston for her singing lesson. She would probably be rehearsing "The Fisherman" for the ceremony less than two weeks away. Mrs. Munger's conservatory was on the fourth floor of the Warren Building on Park Street near Boston Common. At 10:50 a.m., Carrie entered the elevator of the building, and shortly after, Walter Jansen was seen climbing the stairs.

Carrie was in the reception room waiting for her lesson to begin while Mrs. Munger was in the classroom teaching some other young women. Mrs. Munger and her pupils heard a frightened cry come from the reception room: "Don't shoot me, Walter. I can't help it." A pistol shot was the only reply. The women screamed as three more shots were fired in quick succession. A long, moaning sound, a cry of misery, could be heard from the other room, losing intensity as strength left the body of Carrie Andrews.

After hearing another body hit the floor, Mrs. Munger tried to open the door but found it locked. She rushed into the hall and down the stairs, calling to the janitor that someone in her room had been shot. The janitor ran outside and found a police officer on the corner of Park and Tremont, and then the two men hurried to the fourth floor and forced the door open.

In the words of the *Boston Daily Globe*: "The tasty little reception room had been suddenly transformed into a most sanguinary picture of ruthless slaughter." Carrie Andrews lay on the floor between two tables against the opposite wall. She had been shot once in the left temple and again in the left cheek, breaking her jaw. Gasping faintly for breath, Carrie was just barely alive when the men entered. A doctor was sent for, but Carrie died shortly after he arrived.

Lying beside her, his feet nearly touching hers, was the body of Walter Jansen. He had two self-inflicted gunshot wounds—one in the back of the head and one to the face. He had also severed an artery in his left wrist. Next to him laid a .38-caliber revolver and a bloody straight razor.

The funeral of Carrie Lowe Andrews was held at the Universalist Church in Essex on February 6, 1894. Mourners came by train and sleigh from

36

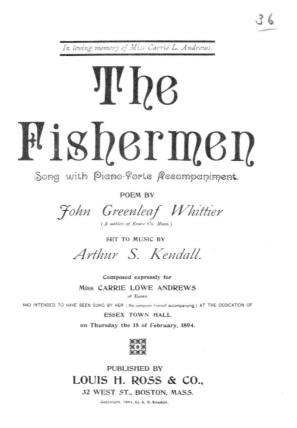

Cover of the sheet music for "The Fisherman."
Courtesy Kurt Wilhelm.

Gloucester, Manchester, Salem, Beverly, Wenham, Hamilton and Ipswich. As many as possible were seated in the church, and hundreds more braved inclement weather to stand in the street outside. Carrie's body, wearing a pink dress, lay in an open casket in front of the church—positioned on her side to hide the disfiguring wounds. The casket was surrounded by dozens of floral tributes. A quartet sang "Nearer My God to Thee," and a soloist sang "One Sweetly Solemn Thought." The ceremony included prayers, scripture readings, a poem and a beautiful eulogy delivered by Reverend George J. Sanger of the Universalist Church, stressing Carrie's purity and nobleness, with no mention of her murder. At 4:00 p.m., the casket was carried to the Spring Street cemetery in a procession led by members of her high school graduating class. Members of Carrie's class also served as pallbearers.

Walter Jansen was buried in Mount Hope Cemetery in Boston. The mental prayers of his grief-stricken brother Hans were the only services.

The T.O.H.P. Burnham Town Hall and Library was dedicated as scheduled, on February 15, 1894. Though the ceremony was upbeat, celebrating the beautiful new building and the seventy-fifth anniversary of the founding of the town of Essex, it was also a gentle memorial to Carrie Lowe Andrews. A portrait of Carrie, sketched by Gilman Lowe, hung on the front of the speaker's desk. The song "The Fisherman," now dedicated to the memory of Carrie Andrews, was sung by Miss Jessie W. Lowe.

More than one hundred years later, the T.O.H.P. Burnham Library still stands on Martin Street in Essex. It still serves its original purposes as library and Essex Town Hall.

BREAKHEART HILL

SAUGUS, 1900

On October 17, 1900, while walking across Floating Bridge on the turnpike between Salem and Lynn, James English and Fred Torrance noticed a cloth bag floating on the westerly side of the bridge. They pulled it to the side, and one of the men took a knife and cut open the bag to see what was inside. It appeared to be a man's shoulder, wearing a striped shirt, an undershirt and suspenders. They cut through the shirts and found human flesh. English and Torrance rushed to Lynn and returned with a policeman, Officer Flynn, who used a pair of ice tongs to pull the bag onto the bridge. He opened the bag and inside found a headless, limbless human torso, with two bullet holes in the chest. More Lynn policemen arrived at the bridge, and using poles and hooks, they brought up several more bags, weighted down with stones, containing arms, legs, a head and the axe that had apparently been used to severe them from the body.

Floating Bridge Pond would be an ideal place to dump a body—if it was sufficiently weighted—because local legend said it had no bottom. In 1803, engineers designing a bridge across what was then called Collins Pond could find no solid bottom, so they built America's first pontoon bridge. It was called Floating Bridge, and the pond was renamed Floating Bridge Pond. The bridge grew thicker and thicker as time went on, because when the surface became old and rotten, a new one was built over it. Although a heavy wagon would splash water up over the sides of the bridge, and circus elephants absolutely refused to cross it, Floating Bridge was part of the Boston-Salem Turnpike for 120 years.

Discovering the body of George E. Bailey. *By Tom Wilhelm.*

1905 postcard of Floating Bridge. *Author's collection.*

The police suspected that the dismembered body found in the pond was that of George E. Bailey, who had disappeared without a trace nine days earlier. Bailey had been the manager of Breakheart Hill, a Saugus farm owned by three Lynn businessmen. The owners had been distressed by

Bailey's disappearance because the man now in charge of the farm, John C. Best, they knew to be an unreliable drunk.

In the late 1890s, three prosperous men of Lynn, Massachusetts—an attorney, a shoe manufacturer and a businessman—formed an association to purchase Breakheart Hill. They had no intention of farming it themselves; it was an investment with benefits. They were speculating that the land would appreciate in value, but it had a considerable amount of tillable land that could be leased to someone who was interested in farming, and it included about three hundred acres of woodland with a camp that the three families would share for recreation. They contracted George E. Bailey, who agreed to rent the farmland for forty dollars per year and do general caretaking to the farm and camp, paid at a rate of twenty cents an hour.

George E. Bailey had come to Saugus from Maine with a woman named Susie L. Young in about 1896. George and Susie lived together as husband and wife, but they were not married. The neighbors were aware of this arrangement but gave it no thought. Bailey was a good, hardworking man, and the rest was none of their business. About a year after moving into Breakheart Hill, Susie Young gave birth to George Bailey's child. What the neighbors did not know was that Susie Young was the half sister of George Bailey's true wife, who was back in Maine raising his other six children.

Bailey had realized early on that one man alone could not do the work necessary to make Breakheart Hill profitable. He brought in a number of different temporary hired hands to help with the farming. One in particular had impressed him, a farmhand named John C. Best, and he went to Best with a proposition: if Best would help with the cultivation of the cash crops, he would receive 50 percent of the profits when they were sold. Bailey would tend to the cows, pigs and chickens and keep that profit for himself. Best agreed, provided that the deal included room and board.

The farm at Breakheart Hill included a small house, a barn, a shed and several small outbuildings. Best was given a room on the second floor of the farmhouse that could be accessed without going through the living area on the first floor. Susie cooked the meals and did the housekeeping, and they all ate together in the kitchen.

John Best was born and raised in New Brunswick, Canada. As a child, he had done farm work and had also become an award-winning marksman. About 1891, when Best was twenty-six years old, his married sister Nettie, who was living in Lynn, Massachusetts, returned for a visit to New Brunswick to show off her new baby. She told her brother of employment opportunities in Lynn and persuaded him to accompany her back to

Massachusetts. Lynn at the time was a leading city in the manufacture of shoes, and while living with his sister and her husband, Best found a job at J.B. Renton's, a heel manufacturer, and worked there for seven or eight years. But Best had a temper, and he spent four months in the Salem House of Correction for assault.

After his release from prison, Best worked some temporary jobs and then went back to work for J.B. Renton's. He had worked there four or five months when three men quit their jobs in a dispute over wages. When their replacements were hired at a reduced rate, the whole shop went out on strike in sympathy with the men who had quit. It was at that point that Best went to Breakheart Hill looking for farm work.

The arrangement worked well for a time; the three appeared to live together in harmony, but away from the farm, Best would complain that he was not being paid all he was entitled to and that Bailey abused the animals that were in his charge. Bailey would complain that Best was lazy and could not be trusted with money. Best appeared to have a drinking problem, and Bailey said he would not pay Best any money until after the crops were sold to keep him from drinking up his share. He would also give him less than was requested for farm expenses because of Best's tendency to take any money he had directly to the saloon.

In September 1900, Susie Young took the child and went back to Maine. Ostensibly it was a visit back home, but everyone knew she was leaving for good. Before she left, she asked John Best if she could write to him. He said yes but told her to send the letters to his sister's address in Lynn because Bailey picked up the mail in Saugus and might not look kindly on a letter from Susie to Best. Following her departure, she did write to John Best but wrote no letters to George Bailey.

After Susie left, relations became increasingly strained between Bailey and Best. Bailey had been three years behind in

Susie L. Young. Boston Daily Globe, *October 19, 1900.*

paying his rent to the owners, but they liked the work he had been doing on the farm and decided to forgive the rent in exchange for the caretaking work he did. Best viewed this as $120 income, of which he deserved $60. He was also displeased with the money he was given for expenses and told anyone who would listen.

The evening of October 8, 1900, proceeded as on any other workday. At about eight o'clock, Bailey harnessed his dark bay horse to an old democrat wagon—a light, four-wheeled farm vehicle—to deliver the day's production of milk to Mr. Deery, a milk dealer. Baily made the same run every working night—down Forest Street to the Newburyport Turnpike. People who lived along the route were familiar with the rattle of the old wagon. Miss Hawkes, who lived on Forrest Street with her niece, would sometimes come to the road at the sound of Bailey's wagon and buy milk from him by the pint or quart. While she did not buy milk from him that night, Mrs. Hawkes heard the wagon rattle past her house several times. In addition to Bailey's milk run, at about ten or eleven o'clock she heard the wagon go past her house again, and at about midnight she heard it return. There was no place it could have come from or returned to but Breakheart Hill.

The same rattling wagon was heard coming out of Lynn Woods sometime after eleven o'clock, heading toward Floating Bridge Pond. A Mrs. Gowen and her husband, who lived near the pond, heard the rattling wagon, driving at a furious pace, pass their house heading toward the bridge.

The next morning, John Best came out of his room as usual and began doing his chores, but George Bailey failed to emerge from the house that morning. Best said he went into the house and into Bailey's room, but Bailey was not there. Best began asking neighbors if they knew what had become of George Bailey.

Micajah Clough, a member of the association that owned Breakheart Hill, got wind of the story of Bailey's disappearance and also heard that Best was constantly drunk, leaving the livestock untended. He went down to see for himself, and Best told him he thought that Bailey was fleeing officers from Maine. There was a $500 reward on Bailey, he said, because he had run out on his wife. In the farmhouse, Clough noticed a rifle that had been provided to the house by the associates hanging on the kitchen wall damp. He told Best it should not have been hung up in that condition.

After the body was found in Floating Bridge Pond, Lynn policemen went to Breakheart Hill to talk to John Best. They explained what they had found, saying they needed Best to come and identify the body. Best agreed to go with them, but in the presence of the officers, Best pulled out a half-full pint of whiskey and downed it before they left the farm. When shown the clothing and remains, Best, now clearly intoxicated, was unable to identify anything. John Best was then arrested for the murder of George Bailey.

John C. Best would be the first Essex County murder defendant to face the possibility of execution by the electric chair. All capital crimes in Massachusetts had been punished by hanging until 1900, when Massachusetts became the third state to adopt electrocution for capital punishment. The electric chair was first envisioned by Alfred P. Southwick, who had seen a man die of electrocution and saw his death to be quick and painless. Southwick believed electrocution would be a humane alternative to hanging, which had unpredictable and often horrendous results, ranging from slow strangulation to decapitation.

The first execution by electrocution was anything but humane. On August 6, 1890, William Kemmler, a convicted axe murderer from Buffalo, New York, was strapped into the new electric chair at the prison in Auburn, New York. After the first seventeen-second jolt of electricity, Kemmler's heart was still beating and he was still breathing. The force was raised to two thousand volts, and he was given a seventy-second jolt. Kemmler began thrashing and convulsing. He was bleeding through the skin, and his body caught fire, filling the room with the smell of burning flesh. Many of the viewers found it necessary to leave the room before Kemmler finally died.

Most of the following New York electrocutions were uneventful, and in 1900, Massachusetts installed an electric chair in Charlestown Prison. From then on, all executions would take place in Charlestown rather than the county in which the murder occurred. The first Massachusetts murderer to face the electric chair was Luigi Storti, who killed his roommate in Boston's North End. Though the U.S. Supreme Court had determined ten years earlier that the electric chair did not violate the Eighth Amendment, Storti's lawyers challenged electrocution on the grounds that it was cruel and unusual, in violation of Article 26 of the Massachusetts Declaration of Rights. Massachusetts chief justice Oliver Wendell Holmes replied, "The suggestion that the punishment of death, in order not to be unusual, must be accomplished by molar rather than molecular motion seems to us a fancy unwarranted by the constitution." Storti was electrocuted.

John C. Best was charged with four counts of murder, one for each bullet fired into George Bailey, one for killing him with an axe and one for killing him with an unknown weapon in an unknown manner. It was a formality— both bullets went through the heart, and the first shot almost certainly killed him. The prosecution wanted to make sure it was covered in the unlikely event that the defense raised doubts about the order of events. The wording of the indictment was meticulously detailed and somewhat archaic for 1900, attempting to explain the mechanics of firearms:

> *John C. Best a certain gun, otherwise called a rifle, then and there charged with gunpowder and one leaden bullet, then and there feloniously, willfully and of his malice aforethought did discharge and shoot off, to, against and upon the said George E. Bailey; and the said John C. Best, with the leaden bullet aforesaid, out of the gun aforesaid, then and there by the force of gunpowder aforesaid, by the said John C. Best discharged and shot off as aforesaid, then and there feloniously, willfully and of his malice aforethought did strike, penetrate and wound the said George E. Bailey in and upon the chest of the body of George E. Bailey, giving to the said George E. Bailey then and there, with the leaden bullet aforesaid, so the aforesaid discharged and shot out of the gun aforesaid by the said John C. Best, in and upon the chest of the body of the said George E Bailey one mortal wound, of which said wound the said George E. Bailey instantly died.*

The trial of John C. Best was held in Salem, beginning March 18, 1901, and continuing for ten days. Seven and a half days were taken up by the prosecution, which called fifty-five witnesses, including Susie Young, who agreed to come down from Maine for the trial.

The prosecution contended that Best knew that, upon returning from his milk delivery, George Bailey would go to the barn, fasten the door from the inside and leave through a door to the cellar of the barn. The night of October 8, Best was waiting for him outside the cellar door with a .38-caliber Winchester rifle that usually hung on the kitchen wall. When Bailey came through the door, Best shot him twice through the heart, the holes less than an inch and a half apart. He put the body on two horse blankets from the barn, and then, using an axe and a large knife that he carried, Best cut off Bailey's head, chopped off his arms just below the shoulders and chopped off his legs above the knees. He put the body parts in some empty cloth grain bags labeled "Estes," a feed store in Saugus Center. Bailey was the only customer that Estes had in that locality. He put the axe in one of the bags and added some rocks from a stone wall for weight.

Best then loaded the bags into the old democrat wagon and left the farm, following the same route Bailey took to Deery's but continuing on down the Newburyport Turnpike to Lynn Woods Road. He then traveled at a furious rate to Floating Bridge Pond and onto the bridge, stopping at a point almost at the end of the bridge, where he dropped the weighted bags into the water. He then hurried back the same way he had come. Back at the farm, Best built a fire and burned the horse blankets and other incriminating evidence.

Many of the witnesses were called to testify about that wagon ride. Those near the farm remembered hearing the distinctive rattle of Bailey's democrat wagon passing their homes around eleven o'clock and then returning an hour later. Those near the pond were not familiar with the sound but remembered hearing a wagon traveling at breakneck speed onto the bridge and then returning. Others were called to relate incriminating statements made by Best before the murder and his suspicious behavior after George Bailey's disappearance. They also introduced ballistic evidence, novel for the time, comparing the markings on the bullets found in the body with others fired from the Winchester rifle.

The defense attorney tried to exploit the medical examiner's inability to accurately pinpoint the time of death. George Bailey disappeared on October 8, and the body was not found until October 18. If the body had been dumped in the pond any day but the eighth, the prosecution's case would fall apart. He challenged the speculative nature of the evidence that did not tightly tie Best to the crime. But he also opened a door for the jury to find Best guilty of second-degree murder. Referring to Best's drinking habits, he explained that while drunkenness is not an excuse for murder, it would tend to rule out premeditation.

John Best testified in his own defense, another new feature in Massachusetts criminal trials. He denied that there was ever bad blood between him and George Bailey and explained away some minor points. The rifle, for example, was damp and recently fired because he had taken it out to show it to one of the boys who occasionally worked on the farm. The cross-examination of Best was severe and lasted longer than the direct. It was here that Best revealed that he had told Susie Young to write to him at his sister's address.

The case was given to the jury on March 28. They deliberated for six hours and then pronounced John C. Best guilty of murder in the first degree. The case was appealed, but the verdict was upheld, and Best was sentenced to be executed.

At midnight on September 9, 1902, John C. Best walked coolly and quietly to the death chair and "sat down composedly as one would waiting for a train at a station." He would not say a word or utter a groan to the end. In a process now familiar to executioners, he was given an initial shock of

JOHN H. BEST,
As He Appeared in Lynn Court This Morning.

Boston Daily Globe,
October 18, 1900.

eleven amperes at 1,750 volts, gradually reduced over the course of thirty seconds. This was repeated twice, and at twenty-two minutes after midnight, John C. Best was dead.

Today, Breakheart Hill is part of Breakheart Reservation, a Massachusetts state park composed of 640 wooded acres and two lakes. It is used primarily for fishing and hiking. The pond where George Bailey's body was found is still called Floating Bridge Pond, but the floating bridge is gone. The bottom of the pond was found, and in 1923, Buchanan Bridge, a concrete bridge built on pilings, was opened to the public.

BIBLIOGRAPHY

BOOKS

Babson, John J., and Samuel Chandler. *History of the Town of Gloucester, Cape Ann Including the Town of Rockport.* Gloucester, MA: Proctor Bros., 1860.

Bailey, Sarah Loring. *Historical Sketches of Andover, (comprising the present towns of North Andover and Andover), Massachusetts.* Boston: Houghton Mifflin, 1880.

Best, John Courtney. *The Official Report of the Trial of John C. Best for Murder.* Boston: Published by the Attorney-General, 1903.

Bradley, T.E. *The Lamp.* Vol. 16. London, 1884.

Caverly, Robert Boodey. *Heroism of Hannah Duston, Together with the Indian Wars of New England.* Boston: Russell, 1874.

Chase, George Wingate. *The History of Haverhill, Massachusetts From its First Settlement, in 1640, to the Year 1860.* Haverhill, MA: self-published, 1861.

Citizen of Danvers. *A Biographical Sketch of the Celebrated Salem Murderer, Who for Ten Years Has Been the Terror of Essex County, Mass. Including a Full and Authentic Account of His Daring Exploits; Together with Many New and Interesting Particulars of the Late Murder.* Boston: self-published, 1830.

Coffin, Joshua, and Joseph Bartlett. *A Sketch of the History of Newbury, Newburyport, and West Newbury, from 1635 to 1845.* Boston: S.G. Drake, 1845.

Colonial Society of Massachusetts. *Publications of the Colonial Society of Massachusetts, Vol. III.* Boston: Colonial Society of Massachusetts, 1900.

Currier, John J. *History of Newbury, Mass., 1635–1902.* Boston: Damrell & Upham, 1902.

————. *History of Newburyport, Mass., 1764–1905*. Newburyport, MA: self-published, 1906.

Dow, George Francis, and John Henry Edmonds. *The Pirates of the New England Coast, 1630–1730*. Salem, MA: Marine Research Society, 1923.

Drake, Samuel Adams. *A Book of New England Legends and Folk Lore in Prose and Poetry*. New and rev. ed., Boston: Little, Brown and Company, 1901.

Duke, Thomas S. *Celebrated Criminal Cases of America*. San Francisco: J.H. Barry, 1910.

The Essex Antiquarian, 1903.

Felt, Joseph B. *History of Ipswich, Essex, and Hamilton*. Ipswich, MA: Clamshell Press, 1966.

Gage, Thomas, and James Bradford. *The History of Rowley, Anciently Including Bradford, Boxford, and Georgetown, from the Year 1639 to the Present Time*. Boston: F. Andrews, 1840.

Goodwin, Henry K., and J.M.W. Yerrinton. *The Official Report of the Trial of Henry K. Goodwin for the Murder of Albert D. Swan in the Supreme Judicial Court of Massachusetts*. Boston: Wright & Potter Co., State Printers, 1887.

Guiley, Rosemary. *The Encyclopedia of Witches and Witchcraft*. New York: Facts on File, 1989.

Hambleton, Else L. *Daughters of Eve: Pregnant Brides and Unwed Mothers in Seventeenth-Century Massachusetts*. New York: Routledge, 2004.

Hamblin, P.R. *United States Criminal History, Being a True Account of the Most Horrid Murders, Piracies, High-way Robberies, &c., Together with the Lives, Trials, Confessions and Executions of the Criminals: Compiled from the Criminal Records of the Counties*. Fayetteville, NY: Mason & De Puy, 1836.

Holliday, Carl. *Woman's Life in Colonial Days*. Williamstown, MA: Corner House, 1968.

Hurd, D. Hamilton. *History of Essex County, Massachusetts: With Biographical Sketches of Many of Its Pioneers and Prominent Men*. Salem, MA: Higginson Book Co., 1987.

Jones, Ann. *Women Who Kill*. New York: Holt, Rinehart, and Winston, 1980.

Kimball, Henrietta D. *Witchcraft Illustrated Witchcraft to Be Understood. Facts, Theories and Incidents. With a Glance at Old and New Salem and Its Historical Resources*. Boston: G.A. Kimball, 1892.

Knapp, John Francis, and Raymond S. Wilkins. *Trial of John Francis Knapp for the Murder of Capt. Joseph White of Salem, on the Night of the 6th of April, 1830*. Brattleboro, VT: Geo. W. Nichols, 1830.

Lawson, John Davison. *American State Trials: A Collection of the Important and Interesting Criminal Trials Which Have Taken Place in the United States from the*

Beginning of our Government to the Present Day. St. Louis, MO: Thomas Law Books, 1914.

Leary, Timothy. *Transactions of the Massachusetts Medico-Legal Society.* Vol. III. Boston: self-published, 1899.

Lewis, Alonzo. *The History of Lynn, Including Nahant.* 2nd ed. Boston: printed by S.N. Dickinson, 1844.

Mather, Cotton. *Magnalia Christi Americana: Or the Ecclesiastical History of New England from 1620–1698.* Hartford, CT: Silas Andrus & Son, 1853.

McDade, Thomas M. *The Annals of Murder: A Bibliography of Books and Pamphlets on American Murders from Colonial Times to 1900.* Norman: University of Oklahoma Press, 1961.

Nelson, Liz. *Newburyport: Stories from the Waterside.* Beverly, MA: Commonwealth Editions, 2000.

Perley, Sidney. *The History of Boxford, Essex County, Massachusetts from the Earliest Settlement Known to the Present Time, a Period of About Two Hundred and Thirty Years.* Boxford, MA: self-published, 1880.

Phillips, John C. *Wenham Great Pond.* Salem, MA: Peabody Museum, 1938.

Pierce, Frederick Clifton. *Forbes and Forbush Genealogy: The Descendants of Daniel Forbush, Who Comes from Scotland about the Year 1655, and Settled in Marlborough, Mass., in 1675.* Chicago: self-published, 1903.

Roach, Marilynne K. *The Salem Witch Trials: A Day-by-Day Chronicle of a Community Under Siege.* New York: Cooper Square Press, 2002.

Rogers, Alan. *Murder and the Death Penalty in Massachusetts.* Amherst: University of Massachusetts Press, 2008.

Sewall, Samuel. *Diary of Samuel Sewall 1674–1729.* Boston: Massachusetts Historical Society, 1878.

Snow, Edward Rowe. *Piracy, Mutiny, and Murder.* New York: Dodd, Mead, 1959.

Specifications and Drawings of Patents Issued from the United States Patent Office. May 30, 1871–June, 1912. Washington, D.C.: Government Office, 1872.

Starkey, Marion Lena. *The Devil in Massachusetts: A Modern Enquiry into the Salem Witch Trials.* New York: Anchor Books, 1989.

Thomson, George Newton. *Confessions, Trials, and Biographical Sketches of the Most Cold Blooded Murderers, who have been Executed in this Country: From Its First Settlement Down to the Present Time: Compiled Entirely from the Most Authentic Sources: Containing also, Accounts.* Hartford, CT: S. Andrus and Son, 1837.

Thoreau, Henry David, and Carl Hovde. *A Week on the Concord and Merrimack Rivers.* Princeton, NJ: Princeton University Press, 1980.

Valentine, Rebecca, and Travis Thompson. *Beyond the Land of Gold: The Life and Times of Perry A. Burgess.* Acworth, GA: Thompson Media, 2010.

Wadsworth, H.A. *Quarter-Centennial History of Lawrence, Massachusetts: With Portraits and Biographical Sketches*. Salem, MA: Higginson Book Co., 1993.

Waters, Thomas Franklin. *A Sketch of the Life of John Winthrop the Younger, Founder of Ipswich, Massachusetts, in 1633*. Cambridge, MA, 1899.

Waters, Thomas Franklin, Sarah Goodhue and John Wise. *Ipswich in the Massachusetts Bay Colony*. Ipswich, MA: Ipswich Historical Society, 1905.

Watts, Joshua. *The Museum of Remarkable and Interesting Events, Containing Historical and other Accounts*. Improved and enl. ed. Cleveland, OH: Sanford & Hayward, 1844.

Webster, Daniel, and Edward Everett. *The Works of Daniel Webster*. Boston: C.C. Little and J. Brown, 1851.

Whittier, John Greenleaf, and John B. Pickard. *Legends of New England (1831)*. Gainesville, FL: Scholar's Facsimiles & Reprints, 1965.

Winthrop, John. *The History of New England from 1630 to 1649*. Boston: Phelps and Farnham, 1825.

NEWSPAPERS

Boston Daily Globe, February 3, 1894.
———, February 6, 1894.
———, February 7, 1894.
———, February 13, 1894.
———, February 16, 1894.
———, July 30, 1897.
———, August 7, 1897.
———, February 8, 1898.
———, February 9, 1898.
———, February 10, 1898.
———, February 11, 1898.
———, February 12, 1898.
———, October 10, 1900.
———, March 29, 1901.
———, September 9, 1902.
Lowell Sun, February 10, 1898.
———, October 7, 1898.
New York Times, February 3, 1894.

WEBSITES

Breakheart Reservation. Wikipedia. en.wikipedia.org/wiki/Breakheart_Reservation.

John Adams. Wikipedia. en.wikipedia.org/wiki/John_Adams.

Kearney, Peg Goggin. "'They Die in Youth and Their Life Is Among the Unclean': The Life and Death of Elizabeth Emerson." wprokasy.myweb.uga.edu/Emerson2.htm.

"Pomp, d. 1795 and Jonathan Plummer, 1761–1819." docsouth.unc.edu/neh/pomp/summary.html.

Puritan Capital Punishment. www.celebrateboston.com/crime/puritan-capital-punishment.htm.

Rachel Wall. www.thepirateking.com/bios/wall_rachel.htm.

Slavery in Massachusetts. www.slavenorth.com/massachusetts.htm.

The Story of Thomas and Hannah Duston/Duston of Haverhill, Massachusetts. www.hannahdustin.com/index2.html.

"Town of Essex." www.rootsweb.ancestry.com/~macessex.

"The Trial and Conviction of John Francis Knapp." toolsofhistory.org/contentdm/cdm4/item_viewer.php?CISOROOT=/p403501document&CISOPTR=322&CISOBOX=1&REC=3

Waters, Wendell. "Chief Masconomet: Lasting Presence in a Changed World." www.wickedlocal.com/hamilton/news/lifestyle/celebrations/x993966829/Chief-Masconomet-Lasting-presence-in-a-changed-world#axzz1PyJJTNhG.

PICTURES

Original drawings, Tom Wilhelm, www.tom-wilhelm.com.

Original photographs, Peter Meo, www.petermeophotography.com.

Painting, *Joseph White*, by Benjamin Blyth. Courtesy of the Peabody Essex Museum, Salem, MA.

ABOUT THE AUTHOR

Robert Wilhelm writes about historical true crime for the blogs "Murder by Gaslight" (www.MurderByGaslight.com) and the "National Night Stick" (www.Night-Stick.com). His interest in historic murders began with the research of traditional American murder ballads, and among the hundred or so murder tales at "Murder by Gaslight" are the true stories behind two dozen murderous folk songs. Together with his wife, Anne, Robert founded—and for fifteen years hosted—the Essex Music Festival, an annual festival of folk and acoustic music on the banks of Chebacco Lake in Essex, Massachusetts.

Visit us at
www.historypress.net